SAVING ENDANGERED SPECIES

THE
CHIMPANZEE

Help Save This Endangered Species!

Stephen Feinstein

MyReportLinks.com Books

an imprint of

 Enslow Publishers, Inc.

Box 398, 40 Industrial Road
Berkeley Heights, NJ 07922
USA

MyReportLinks.com Books, an imprint of Enslow Publishers, Inc. MyReportLinks®
is a registered trademark of Enslow Publishers, Inc.

Library of Congress Cataloging-in-Publication Data

Feinstein, Stephen.
  The chimpanzee: help save this endangered species! / Stephen Feinstein.
    p. cm. — (Saving endangered species)
  Includes bibliographical references (p.   ) and index.
  ISBN-13: 978-1-59845-039-2
  ISBN-10: 1-59845-039-5
  1. Chimpanzees—Juvenile literature. I. Title.
QL737.P96F45 2007
599.885—dc22

                                        2006028079

Printed in the United States of America

10 9 8 7 6 5 4 3 2 1

To Our Readers:
Through the purchase of this book, you and your library gain access to the Report Links that specifically
back up this book.
The Publisher will provide access to the Report Links that back up this book and will keep these Report
Links up to date on **www.myreportlinks.com** for five years from the book's first publication date.
We have done our best to make sure all Internet addresses in this book were active and appropriate when
we went to press. However, the author and the Publisher have no control over, and assume no liability
for, the material available on those Internet sites or on other Web sites they may link to.
The usage of the MyReportLinks.com Books Web site is subject to the terms and conditions stated on the
Usage Policy Statement on **www.myreportlinks.com.**
A password may be required to access the Report Links that back up this book. The password is found
on the bottom of page 4 of this book.
Any comments or suggestions can be sent by e-mail to comments@myreportlinks.com or to the address
on the back cover.

Photo Credits: ©ecliptic blue/Shutterstock.com, p. 1; ©Tony Campbell/Shutterstock.com, p. 109;
Animal Planet, p. 34; Australian Museum, p. 71; Brand X Pictures, pp. 47, 53; Chimp Haven, p. 95;
Chimpanzee SSP, Lincoln Park Zoo, p. 44; ChimpanZoo, p. 40; Columbus Zoo and Aquarium, p. 30;
Defenders of Wildlife, p. 32; Enslow Publishers, Inc., p. 5; Friends of Washoe, p. 103; Getty Images,
pp. 10, 36, 39, 42–43, 50–51, 55, 60, 62, 64–65, 67, 78, 96, 98, 104, 115; International Primate
Protection League, p. 92; Library of Congress, pp. 69, 73; MyReportLinks.com Books, p. 4; *National
Geographic Kids,* p. 94; Palomar College, p. 29; PBS, p. 12; Photograph by Hugo Van Lawick, courtesy of
the Jane Goodall Institute, www.janegoodall.org., p. 83; Project Primate, Inc., p. 21; Save the Chimps,
p. 23; The Animal Legal Defense Fund, p. 114; The Chimpanzee and Human Communication Institute,
p. 106; The Fauna Foundation, p. 19; The Great Ape Project, p. 116; The Jane Goodall Institute for
Wildlife Research, Education and Conservation, pp. 15, 17, 25; The Jane Goodall Institute's Center for
Primate Studies, University of Minnesota, p. 87; The Leakey Foundation, p. 85; The University of
Michigan, p. 91; The Wildlife Conservation Society, p. 113; Tufts University, p. 100; U.S. Fish and Wildlife
Service, pp. 13, 117; United States House of Representatives, p. 26; Voya Pomortzeff/Getty Images, p. 3;
Wolfgang Köhler Primate Research Center, p. 74; World Wildlife Fund, p. 110.

Cover Photo: ©ecliptic blue/Shutterstock.com

CONTENTS

About MyReportLinks.com Books   4

Chimpanzee Range Map   5

Chimpanzee Facts.   6

1 Our Closest Relative   9

2 About Chimpanzees 28

3 Chimpanzee Behavior 38

4 Early Research 68

5 Jane Goodall and the
    Chimpanzees of Gombe 81

6 Chimpanzee-Human Communication 100

7 Current Efforts to Protect
    the Chimpanzee. 110

The Endangered and
    Threatened Wildlife List 117

Report Links 118

Glossary. 120

Chapter Notes. 122

Further Reading 125

Index 126

MyReportLinks.com Books
Great Books, Great Links, Great for Research!

The Internet sites featured in this book can save you hours of research time. These Internet sites—we call them **"Report Links"**—are constantly changing, but we keep them up to date on our Web site.

When you see this "Approved Web Site" logo, you will know that we are directing you to a great Internet site that will help you with your research.

Give it a try! Type http://www.myreportlinks.com into your browser, click on the series title and enter the password, then click on the book title, and scroll down to the Report Links listed for this book.

The Report Links will bring you to great source documents, photographs, and illustrations. MyReportLinks.com Books save you time, feature Report Links that are kept up to date, and make report writing easier than ever! A complete listing of the Report Links can be found on pages 118–119 at the back of the book.

Please see "To Our Readers" on the copyright page for important information about this book, the MyReportLinks.com Web site, and the Report Links that back up this book.

Please enter **CES1256** if asked for a password.

Chimpanzee Range Map

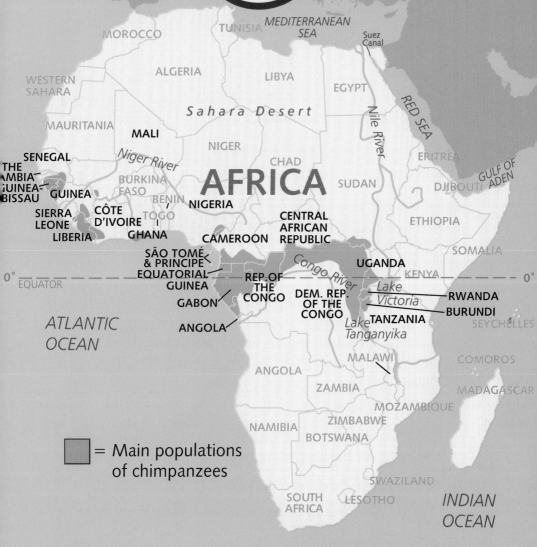

MEDITERRANEAN SEA

MOROCCO
TUNISIA
Suez Canal

WESTERN SAHARA
ALGERIA
LIBYA
EGYPT

RED SEA

MAURITANIA
Sahara Desert
Nile River

MALI
NIGER
CHAD
ERITREA

SENEGAL
Niger River
AFRICA
SUDAN
DJIBOUTI
GULF OF ADEN

THE GAMBIA
GUINEA-BISSAU
GUINEA
BURKINA FASO
BENIN
NIGERIA

SIERRA LEONE
CÔTE D'IVOIRE
TOGO
CENTRAL AFRICAN REPUBLIC
ETHIOPIA

LIBERIA
GHANA
CAMEROON
SOMALIA

SÃO TOMÉ & PRINCIPE
EQUATORIAL GUINEA
Congo River
UGANDA
KENYA

0°
EQUATOR
REP. OF THE CONGO
Lake Victoria
RWANDA
0°

GABON
DEM. REP. OF THE CONGO
BURUNDI

ANGOLA
Lake Tanganyika
TANZANIA
SEYCHELLES

ATLANTIC OCEAN

ANGOLA
MALAWI
COMOROS

ZAMBIA
MADAGASCAR

MOZAMBIQUE

NAMIBIA
ZIMBABWE
BOTSWANA

■ = Main populations of chimpanzees

SWAZILAND

SOUTH AFRICA
LESOTHO
INDIAN OCEAN

CHIMPANZEE FACTS

▶ **Scientific Name**

Pan troglodytes

▶ **Description**

Pinkish to black faces, with bodies covered by long black or dark-brown hair; long arms; no tails; opposable thumbs and toes that aid in grasping. Adult chimpanzees are similar in size to adolescent humans.

▶ **Range**

Wide belt across equatorial Africa, in about twenty-one African countries

▶ **Habitats**

Low-altitude, tropical, humid rain forests; dry wood-lands; savanna grasslands

▶ **Current Estimated Population**

Between 100,000 and 200,000

▶ **Life Span**

Between 35 and 40 years in the wild, 40 to 50 years in captivity

▶ **Size**

Adult males weigh from 90 to 115 pounds (41 to 52 kilograms); adult females weigh 57 to 110 pounds (26 to 50 kilograms). Adult males are 3 to 4 feet (0.9 to 1.2 meters) tall; adult females are 2 to 3.5 feet (0.61 to 1 meter) tall.

▶ **Diet**

Chimpanzees are omnivorous, eating plants and meat, although 60 percent of their diet is made up of fruit.

▶ **Community Organization**

Chimpanzees live in communities made up of as many as fifty animals, in family groups numbering between three and six individuals. Adult males form the community's hierarchy, with an alpha male at the top.

▶ **Sensory Systems**

Similar to humans, but with keener sense of smell

▶ **Locomotion**

Chimpanzees usually walk on all fours, in knuckle-walking, but they can also walk upright on two feet and hang by arms.

▶ **Use of Tools**

Chimpanzees make and use tools, such as twigs to get at insects, hammers made out of stone to crack nuts, and leaves used as sponges to absorb water.

▶ **Communication**

Vocal communication consists of a variety of calls. Physical communication includes grooming, hugging, kissing, and holding hands. Visual communication includes gestures, body postures, and facial expressions. Chimpanzees have been taught to communicate with humans by using American Sign Language (ASL) or symbols.

▶ **Reproduction**

Chimpanzees are full grown at twelve to thirteen years of age and are then able to reproduce. A pregnancy lasts an average of eight months. Mothers usually give birth to a single baby. Chimpanzees may stay with their mothers for up to ten years.

▶ **Threats to Survival**

Loss of habitat to logging and development; hunting for live export and for bush meat; illnesses such as tuberculosis and the Ebola virus

How should we relate to beings who look into mirrors and see themselves as individuals, who mourn companions and may die of grief, who have a consciousness of "self"? Don't they deserve to be treated with the same sort of consideration we accord to other highly sensitive beings: ourselves?

Dr. Jane Goodall

Chapter 1 ▶

OUR CLOSEST RELATIVE

Most of us already know something about chimpanzees. We have seen them in movies, on television, in zoos, and perhaps in circuses. We tend to think of them as smart, cute creatures, and we are amused by their antics. But it is only within the past fifty years that scientists have studied chimpanzees in depth. They have come to appreciate the intelligence of these remarkable animals. They have come to realize just how much chimpanzees resemble human beings. And they have begun to see just how unlike us chimpanzees are in other ways, making it even more important that we preserve their forest and grassland habitat in western and central Africa and allow them to roam free and wild.

▶ The Work of Jane Goodall

Much of what we know today about this species of great ape comes from Dr. Jane Goodall, considered one of the world's leading primatologists, scientists who study primates. Goodall made the study of these animals her life's work. She became the

Chimpanzees, so like us and yet so different, have long captured our imagination.

first scientist to carry out long-term studies of wild chimpanzees in their native African habitat. She lived among them and observed them closely for many years. She has contributed more to our understanding of chimpanzees than any other scientist.

Goodall began studying the chimpanzees in Gombe Stream National Park, in what was then Tanganyika and is now the eastern African country of Tanzania, in July 1960. Later that year, she reported that she saw a chimpanzee using a tool. She observed the chimpanzee, whom she named David Greybeard, fishing for termites using a piece of straw. She also saw a chimpanzee gathering termites with a stick that the chimp had stripped of its leaves. The ability to make and use tools had always been considered one of the main characteristics separating humans from other animals. When the famous anthropologist Louis Leakey heard about Goodall's discovery, he wrote to her, saying, "Now we must redefine *tool*, redefine *man*, or accept chimpanzees as human."[1]

Goodall reported that chimpanzees demonstrated other humanlike behaviors. These included close supportive bonds among family members lasting throughout a lifetime of fifty or more years. Chimpanzees also exhibited complex social interactions such as cooperation, altruism (concern for

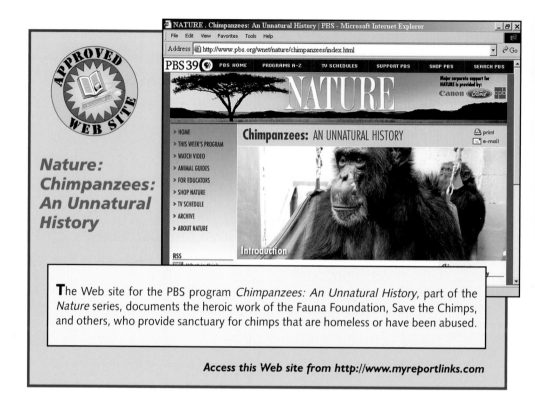

Nature: Chimpanzees: An Unnatural History

NATURE . Chimpanzees: An Unnatural History | PBS - Microsoft Internet Explorer

File   Edit   View   Favorites   Tools   Help

Address   http://www.pbs.org/wnet/nature/chimpanzees/index.html   Go

PBS 39   PBS HOME   PROGRAMS A-Z   TV SCHEDULES   SUPPORT PBS   SHOP PBS   SEARCH PBS

Major corporate support for NATURE is provided by: Canon Ford cpb

NATURE

> HOME
> THIS WEEK'S PROGRAM
> WATCH VIDEO
> ANIMAL GUIDES
> FOR EDUCATORS
> SHOP NATURE
> TV SCHEDULE
> ARCHIVE
> ABOUT NATURE

RSS

Chimpanzees: AN UNNATURAL HISTORY

print   e-mail

Introduction

The Web site for the PBS program *Chimpanzees: An Unnatural History,* part of the *Nature* series, documents the heroic work of the Fauna Foundation, Save the Chimps, and others, who provide sanctuary for chimps that are homeless or have been abused.

Access this Web site from http://www.myreportlinks.com

others), and expressions of emotions like joy and sadness.

Other researchers, including Roger Fouts, have learned that chimpanzees are able to reason, plan for the immediate future, and solve simple problems. Dr. Fouts, a professor of psychology, is the codirector of the Chimpanzee and Human Communication Institute at Central Washington University, which provides sanctuary to an amazing family of chimpanzees that have been taught to communicate with humans—and each other—by using American Sign Language (ASL) symbols.

▶ A Common Ancestor

Perhaps we should not have been surprised to learn that chimpanzees can learn to communicate using abstract symbols. After all, chimpanzees and their cousins, bonobos (also called gracile chimpanzees), are genetically closer to human beings than they are to any other animal, including monkeys. Nearly 99 percent of human and chimpanzee and bonobo DNA is identical, which makes these great apes the closest living relatives to humans. And both humans and chimps have a common ancestor. According to Roger Fouts, "After humans and chimps diverged six million years ago, each

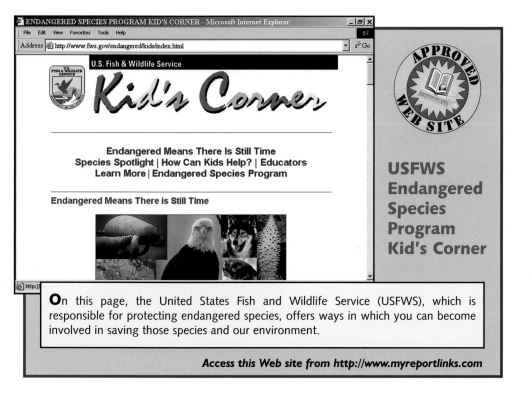

USFWS
Endangered
Species
Program
Kid's Corner

On this page, the United States Fish and Wildlife Service (USFWS), which is responsible for protecting endangered species, offers ways in which you can become involved in saving those species and our environment.

Access this Web site from http://www.myreportlinks.com

species undoubtedly adapted the single system of communication it inherited from a common ancestor to suit its specialized needs."[2]

Threats to the Species

As we learn more about chimpanzees, we also have learned about the threats to their survival. Sadly, the chimpanzee has joined a long and growing list of animals that are now classified as endangered species. In 1973, the United States government officially began making a list of endangered and threatened species. The Endangered Species Act defines an endangered species as one that is in immediate danger of becoming extinct throughout most of its range. Threatened species are defined as those that could become endangered in the near future. Chimpanzees are also protected by international law under the Convention on International Trade in Endangered Species of Wild Fauna and Flora (CITES). Even so, mostly because of the activities of human beings, chimpanzees are losing their habitat, and their numbers are rapidly declining.

As the human population grows larger, the chimpanzees' habitat grows smaller. Loggers and miners cut down trees and build roads through the forest habitat of the chimpanzees. Local people clear the land for farming, firewood, and to build on. Roads built by loggers and others force chimpanzees to live in small areas, which forces

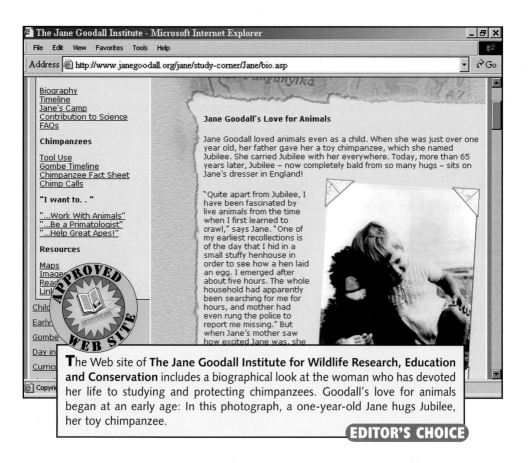

The Jane Goodall Institute - Microsoft Internet Explorer

File   Edit   View   Favorites   Tools   Help

Address 🔲 http://www.janegoodall.org/jane/study-corner/Jane/bio.asp ▾ ⌀ Go

Biography
Timeline
Jane's Camp
Contribution to Science
FAQs

Chimpanzees

Tool Use
Gombe Timeline
Chimpanzee Fact Sheet
Chimp Calls

"I want to. . "

"...Work With Animals"
"...Be a Primatologist"
"...Help Great Apes!"

Resources

Maps
Image
Read
Link

Chil

Early

Gomb

Day i

Curri

Copyri

Jane Goodall's Love for Animals

Jane Goodall loved animals even as a child. When she was just over one year old, her father gave her a toy chimpanzee, which she named Jubilee. She carried Jubilee with her everywhere. Today, more than 65 years later, Jubilee – now completely bald from so many hugs – sits on Jane's dresser in England!

"Quite apart from Jubilee, I have been fascinated by live animals from the time when I first learned to crawl," says Jane. "One of my earliest recollections is of the day that I hid in a small stuffy henhouse in order to see how a hen laid an egg. I emerged after about five hours. The whole household had apparently been searching for me for hours, and mother had even rung the police to report me missing." But when Jane's mother saw how excited Jane was, she

The Web site of **The Jane Goodall Institute for Wildlife Research, Education and Conservation** includes a biographical look at the woman who has devoted her life to studying and protecting chimpanzees. Goodall's love for animals began at an early age: In this photograph, a one-year-old Jane hugs Jubilee, her toy chimpanzee.

EDITOR'S CHOICE

the chimpanzees to be separated into smaller populations. This leads to inbreeding—mating between chimpanzees that are closely related. Although this is not a problem for chimpanzees at present, it could become one.

People also kill chimpanzees for many reasons. Chimp meat is often combined with that of monkeys, antelopes, and other animals to make bush meat. Bush meat, wild animal meat, while illegal, is less expensive than meat from domesticated animals such as cows. People also capture chimpanzee infants to sell as exotic pets or to be used for entertainment. They often kill the chimpanzee mothers in the process. Chimpanzees that raid crops from farms close to their forest habitat are also killed. And in some areas, chimpanzees are killed for use in religious rituals. So unfortunately, for these and other reasons, our closest relatives are in danger of becoming extinct.

How You Can Help

Jane Goodall and other scientists and wildlife experts have dedicated their lives to saving chimpanzees from extinction. But you do not need to be a scientist or a member of a conservation organization to make a difference. There are many ways that you can also help to save chimpanzees from disappearing from the earth forever. Nonprofit organizations dedicated to caring for chimpanzees depend on volunteers and donations to do the work they do.

The organizations involved in helping chimpanzees include the Jane Goodall Institute for Wildlife Research, Education and Conservation; the Fauna Foundation; the Chimpanzee Collaboratory; and Save the Chimps.

The Jane Goodall Institute

The Jane Goodall Institute for Wildlife Research, Education and Conservation not only works to

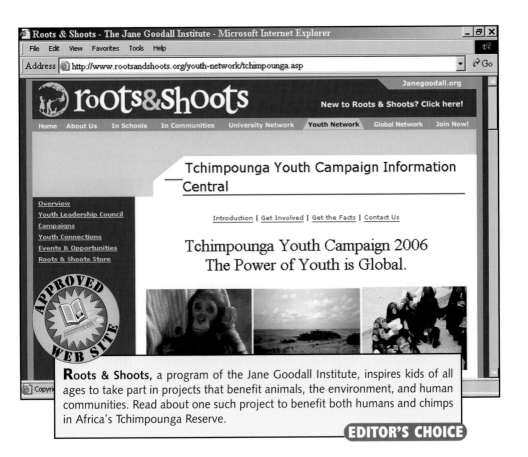

Roots & Shoots - The Jane Goodall Institute - Microsoft Internet Explorer

File   Edit   View   Favorites   Tools   Help

Address   http://www.rootsandshoots.org/youth-network/tchimpounga.asp   Go

Janegoodall.org

roots&shoots

New to Roots & Shoots? Click here!

Home | About Us | In Schools | In Communities | University Network | Youth Network | Global Network | Join Now!

Overview
Youth Leadership Council
Campaigns
Youth Connections
Events & Opportunities
Roots & Shoots Store

Tchimpounga Youth Campaign Information Central

Introduction | Get Involved | Get the Facts | Contact Us

Tchimpounga Youth Campaign 2006
The Power of Youth is Global.

Roots & Shoots, a program of the Jane Goodall Institute, inspires kids of all ages to take part in projects that benefit animals, the environment, and human communities. Read about one such project to benefit both humans and chimps in Africa's Tchimpounga Reserve.

EDITOR'S CHOICE

APPROVED WEB SITE

protect chimpanzees and other primates but is also involved in animal welfare activities in general. In addition, the institute is dedicated to improving education for Africa's children and promoting businesses that help preserve habitat for both animals and people. The institute operates two chimpanzee sanctuaries in Africa, Ngamba and Tchimpounga, although it provides money to other sanctuaries.

With your classmates and teacher, you could become involved in helping chimpanzees by holding a fund-raising activity and donating the proceeds to the Jane Goodall Institute. Your contribution, which makes you a "Chimp Guardian," goes to support research by the institute at the Gombe Stream Research Center and will help the sanctuaries carry out their programs. By becoming a Chimp Guardian, your class receives a biography of the chimpanzee you "adopt," a chimpanzee poster, a certificate of guardianship, and information about the institute, its sanctuary program, and the Gombe Stream Research Center.

▶ An Outgrowth: Roots & Shoots

Jane Goodall also started an educational program called Roots & Shoots. She thought about how the roots of trees form a firm foundation, and although shoots are small, they are strong enough to break apart brick walls to reach the light. To Goodall, the bad things that human beings have done to the environment seemed like a brick wall. With Roots & Shoots, Goodall envisioned young people all around the world breaking through and making the world a better place for all living things. The first Roots & Shoots group was established in Tanzania. Now there are Roots & Shoots groups in fifty countries. In the program, each group chooses at least one hands-on activity in each of the following areas: care and concern for animals, concern for the human community, and concern for the environment. If you are interested in joining or forming a Roots & Shoots group, you can find more information on the Roots & Shoots Web site.

The Fauna Foundation

The Fauna Foundation was founded in 1997 by Gloria Grow, an animal-rights activist, and her partner, Dr. Richard Allan, a veterinarian. They established a sanctuary for chimpanzees on two hundred acres of farmland in Carignan, Quebec, near Montreal. The sanctuary is home to twelve chimpanzees. Many are survivors of years of bio-medical research, where they were used to test

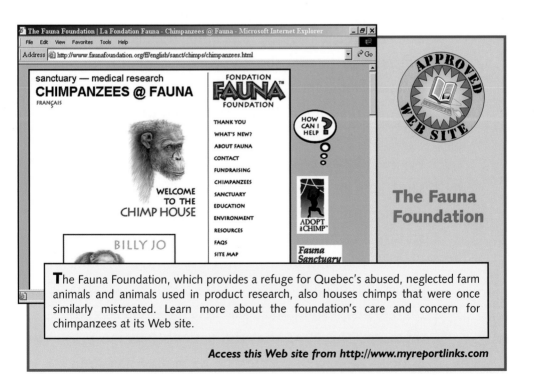

The Fauna Foundation, which provides a refuge for Quebec's abused, neglected farm animals and animals used in product research, also houses chimps that were once similarly mistreated. Learn more about the foundation's care and concern for chimpanzees at its Web site.

Access this Web site from http://www.myreportlinks.com

vaccines before giving the vaccines to humans. They will never be returned to medical labs. But their rehabilitation is more expensive than that of most other chimpanzees. Some of the chimpanzees at the sanctuary had been used in the entertainment industry. Others are discarded pets whose owners could no longer maintain them once they reached adulthood. At the sanctuary, the chimpanzees get to live out their lives in peace.

▶ "Adopt" a Chimp

If you want to help the Fauna Foundation, you can take part in their adopt-a-chimp program. "Adopting" a chimpanzee, which involves sponsoring that chimp's care through a donation, would be an excellent class project. You and your classmates can chip in to pay the one-time fee of fifty-five dollars Canadian. The Fauna Foundation will send you information about the individual chimps. You get to choose from among Yoko, Binky, Sue Ellen, Pepper, or any of the others. The foundation will send you an adoption kit that includes detailed biographical information of your chimpanzee and an official adoption certificate.

The foundation does not encourage private ownership of chimpanzees. Most people who have tried to keep chimpanzees as pets have had to give them up. They find that the animals become too difficult and even dangerous to manage as they

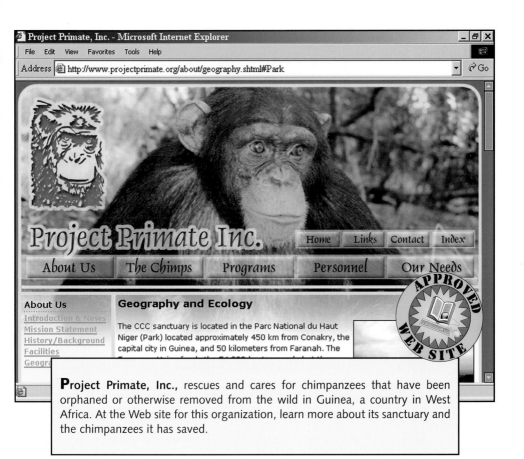

Project Primate, Inc. - Microsoft Internet Explorer

File   Edit   View   Favorites   Tools   Help

Address http://www.projectprimate.org/about/geography.shtml#Park   Go

Project Primate Inc.

Home   Links   Contact   Index

About Us   The Chimps   Programs   Personnel   Our Needs

About Us
Introduction & News
Mission Statement
History/Background
Facilities
Geogra

Geography and Ecology

The CCC sanctuary is located in the Parc National du Haut Niger (Park) located approximately 450 km from Conakry, the capital city in Guinea, and 50 kilometers from Faranah. The

APPROVED WEB SITE

Project Primate, Inc., rescues and cares for chimpanzees that have been orphaned or otherwise removed from the wild in Guinea, a country in West Africa. At the Web site for this organization, learn more about its sanctuary and the chimpanzees it has saved.

grow up. The chimpanzees at the sanctuary cannot be returned to Africa. Most have lived their lives in North America and could not survive in the wild. Also, the natural habitats of chimpanzees in Africa are being destroyed, and sanctuaries in Africa are too crowded to accommodate more chimpanzees.

By adopting a chimp, you help the Fauna Foundation to not only care for the chimps in its own sanctuary but also support the Jane Goodall

Institute's Tchimpounga Sanctuary in Point Noire, Republic of the Congo. The Fauna Foundation also uses monies from adoptions to help Project Primate, which supports the Chimpanzee Conservation Center's rehabilitation sanctuary in the National Park du Haut Niger in Guinea, West Africa. So by participating in the adopt-a-chimp program, you are not only helping support the Fauna Foundation's chimpanzees but also other chimpanzees in their native African habitat.

▶ Save the Chimps

Save the Chimps is another organization that has established a sanctuary for chimpanzees. Founded in 1997 by Carole Noon, Ph.D., the organization established a two-hundred-acre permanent sanctuary on a group of islands in Fort Pierce, Florida, where more than three hundred chimps now live. Its first residents were twenty-one chimpanzees who are either survivors or descendants of those used by the Air Force in NASA's "chimponaut" program. By the 1960s, the United States was no longer launching chimpanzees into space but was conducting medical experiments on them. Save the Chimps rescued more than 266 chimpanzees from the Coulston Foundation's medical labs in Alamogordo, New Mexico. The Coulston labs were forced to close because of their violations of the Animal Welfare Act.

Like the Fauna Foundation, Save the Chimps has an adopt-a-chimp program to raise money for chimpanzee conservation. If you choose one of their chimpanzees, Save the Chimps will send you a photograph of him or her, an official adoption certificate, a biography, and updated information.

Save the Chimps also welcomes the donation of toys that the chimpanzees can play with. If you enjoy creating art, send your drawings and paintings to Save the Chimps. The chimpanzee enclosures have been decorated with children's art. Save the Chimps has done a marvelous job transforming drab enclosures into bright, interesting environments.

The Save the Chimps organization, created in 1997, now operates a sanctuary in Florida for chimpanzees rescued from laboratories. Read more about this organization and its efforts from its Web site.

EDITOR'S CHOICE

Access this Web site from http://www.myreportlinks.com

▶ The Chimpanzee Collaboratory

A group called the Chimpanzee Collaboratory invites you to sign its petition to put an end to the use of baby chimpanzees in the entertainment industry. The group consists of scientists and attorneys working to make progress in protecting the lives and establishing the legal rights of chimpanzees and other great apes. If you go to the group's Web site, you will find this petition:

> You know those funny chimpanzees you see in movies and on TV selling soda or toys? Did you know that these chimpanzees are babies? They don't live with their moms. These babies are asked to do things that they would never choose to do.
>
> Please sign our petition. By adding your name to our list you are telling the people in charge that you will not pay to see these movies and you will not buy the stuff they are trying to sell. These baby chimps miss their moms and that's where they belong.
>
> I agree that chimpanzees don't belong in movies and on TV and I won't pay to go see or watch any movie or show that uses one. I also won't buy any product that uses a chimpanzee to advertise. These babies belong with their mothers, not on TV![3]

After signing the petition, you can ask your friends, classmates, and family members to do the same.

▶ Other Ways to Get Involved

Another way to help protect the chimpanzee is to set up an information table at your school to tell

people about the threat of extinction facing chimpanzees and the other great apes. Gather information about chimpanzees from the organizations mentioned earlier. Use the information to create posters to display at your table. Include a poster with images of the four great apes: the chimpanzee, the bonobo (a separate species of chimpanzee, sometimes called the pygmy chimpanzee), the gorilla, and the orangutan. You can include a graph showing the dramatic decline in the numbers of chimpanzees. The world's chimpanzee population has gone from about one million in 1900 to less then two hundred thousand today.

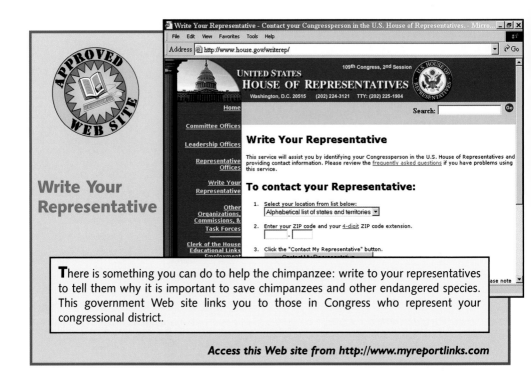

Write Your Representative - Contact your Congressperson in the U.S. House of Representatives. - Micro...

File   Edit   View   Favorites   Tools   Help

Address   http://www.house.gov/writerep/   Go

109th Congress, 2nd Session

UNITED STATES
HOUSE OF REPRESENTATIVES
Washington, D.C. 20515   (202) 224-3121   TTY: (202) 225-1904

Home

Search: Go

Committee Offices

Leadership Offices

Representative Offices

Write Your Representative

Other Organizations, Commissions, & Task Forces

Clerk of the House Educational Links Employment

Write Your Representative

This service will assist you by identifying your Congressperson in the U.S. House of Representatives and providing contact information. Please review the frequently asked questions if you have problems using this service.

To contact your Representative:

1. Select your location from list below:
   Alphabetical list of states and territories

2. Enter your ZIP code and your 4-digit ZIP code extension.

3. Click the "Contact My Representative" button.

Write Your Representative

There is something you can do to help the chimpanzee: write to your representatives to tell them why it is important to save chimpanzees and other endangered species. This government Web site links you to those in Congress who represent your congressional district.

Access this Web site from http://www.myreportlinks.com

You can also become involved in writing letters to your local or school newspaper in support of specific policies to protect chimpanzees. Letters supporting any measures to protect the environment in general, especially policies aimed at reducing the burning of fossil fuels (oil, natural gas, and coal), are also helpful. Most scientists agree that global warming is at least partly caused by our use of those nonrenewable sources of energy. Climate changes due to global warming may also add to the devastation of chimpanzee habitat in Africa caused by human activity.

You can also help protect the chimpanzee by sending a letter or an e-mail in support of the

Endangered Species Act (ESA) to your representative in Congress. The ESA is currently under threat by those in Congress who want to weaken the protections it has provided to endangered animals and their habitats for more than thirty years. A bill, H.R. 2384, titled the *Threatened and Endangered Species Recovery Act of 2005* was passed by the U.S. House of Representatives and referred to the Senate, where it awaits action. While the title of this bill makes is sound as if the legislation would help endangered species, in reality it would remove many of the protections currently afforded them under the existing ESA. In particular, it would do away with establishing critical habitat for species, which is so important to saving those species.

While you are too young to vote now, you can help educate your parents and other adults about the threats to the ESA, so that they can choose to vote for candidates who support environmental issues.

ABOUT CHIMPANZEES

Chimpanzees are mammals, highly developed warm-blooded animals that are covered with hair. Like all other female mammals, the female chimpanzee gives birth to live young and provides milk for her young. The chimpanzee, whose name is often abbreviated to "chimp," is a primate. The primates are a large group of mammals that includes humans, great apes (gorillas, chimpanzees, orangutans, and bonobos), lesser apes (gibbons and siamangs), Old World monkeys (baboons, macaques, and colobus monkeys), New World monkeys (marmosets, tamarins, and capuchins), and prosimians (lemurs, lorises, and tarsiers). Primates were classified as a group in 1758 by the Swedish botanist Carolus Linnaeus.

Sometime during the 1600s, European explorers in Angola made the first Western contact between humans and chimpanzees. Of course, Africans had known about chimpanzees for thousands of years. According to Jane Goodall, "The name *chimpanzee* was first used in the *London Magazine* [in 1738]: 'A most surprising

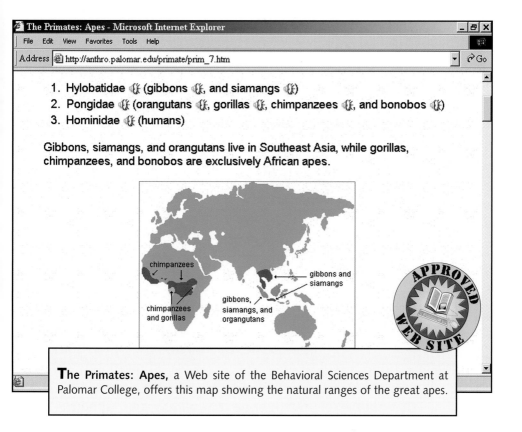

The Primates: Apes - Microsoft Internet Explorer

File   Edit   View   Favorites   Tools   Help

Address http://anthro.palomar.edu/primate/prim_7.htm

1. Hylobatidae (gibbons, and siamangs)
2. Pongidae (orangutans, gorillas, chimpanzees, and bonobos)
3. Hominidae (humans)

Gibbons, siamangs, and orangutans live in Southeast Asia, while gorillas, chimpanzees, and bonobos are exclusively African apes.

The Primates: Apes, a Web site of the Behavioral Sciences Department at Palomar College, offers this map showing the natural ranges of the great apes.

creature is brought over . . . that was taken in a wood in Guinea. She is the female of the creature which the Angolans call chimpanzee, or the mockman.'"[1] The Europeans took the name "chimpanzee" from the Angolan Bantu language term "Tshiluba kivili-chimpenze."

To scientists, the *pan* from *chimpanzee* suggested the god or spirit Pan of Greek mythology. Scientists now refer to chimpanzees as *Pan troglodytes.* According to the ancient Greeks, troglodytes were dwellers in dark caves. *Troglodytes* is the name of the species, and *Pan* is

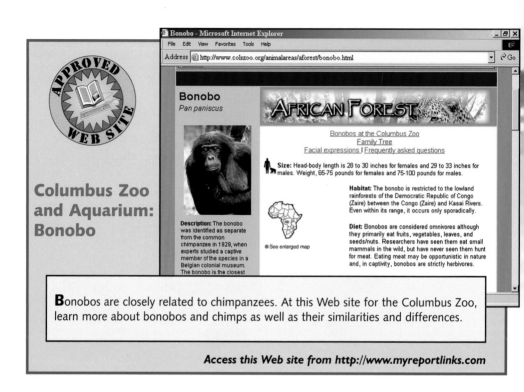

Bonobo - Microsoft Internet Explorer

File   Edit   View   Favorites   Tools   Help

Address   http://www.colszoo.org/animalareas/aforest/bonobo.html

Bonobo
Pan paniscus

AFRICAN FOREST

Bonobos at the Columbus Zoo
Family Tree
Facial expressions I Frequently asked questions

Size: Head-body length is 28 to 30 inches for females and 29 to 33 inches for males. Weight, 65-75 pounds for females and 75-100 pounds for males.

Habitat: The bonobo is restricted to the lowland rainforests of the Democratic Republic of Congo (Zaire) between the Congo (Zaire) and Kasai Rivers. Even within its range, it occurs only sporadically.

Description: The bonobo was identified as separate from the common chimpanzee in 1929, when experts studied a captive member of the species in a Belgian colonial museum. The bonobo is the closest

● See enlarged map

Diet: Bonobos are considered omnivores although they primarily eat fruits, vegetables, leaves, and seeds/nuts. Researchers have seen them eat small mammals in the wild, but have never seen them hunt for meat. Eating meat may be opportunistic in nature and, in captivity, bonobos are strictly herbivores.

Columbus Zoo and Aquarium: Bonobo

Bonobos are closely related to chimpanzees. At this Web site for the Columbus Zoo, learn more about bonobos and chimps as well as their similarities and differences.

Access this Web site from http://www.myreportlinks.com

the name of the genus to which the species belongs.

A species is defined as a group of organisms so similar to one another that they can interbreed. A genus is a group of closely related species. The genus *Pan* consists of two species: *Pan troglodytes,* chimpanzees, and *Pan paniscus,* bonobos. The bonobo, a cousin of the more well-known chimpanzee now sometimes called the robust chimpanzee, has a body about the same size as a chimp's, but it has a smaller head, teeth, and ears. Bonobos have longer arms and walk upright more frequently than chimps do. There are also behavioral differences. Chimpanzees are omnivorous, eating meat as well as plants. Bonobos, on the other hand, are mainly vegetarians.

Chimpanzee Habitat and Distribution

Chimpanzees live in a wide area extending across Africa, near the equator, from the east coast of the continent to the west coast.

Chimpanzees are able to adapt to a far greater variety of habitat than any of the other great apes. Some chimpanzees live in low-altitude, tropical rain forests. Their habitat can include swamp forests, forest edges, and clearings. Here the warm temperatures are fairly constant throughout the year. There may be only a few dry days each year, although some months may be wetter than others. Some chimpanzees inhabit woodlands, while others live in savannas, grasslands with widely scattered trees. Both areas usually have a rainy season and a dry season, although the savannas are drier and hotter because there is less vegetation covering the ground. There is also a much greater range of temperature than in the rain forests. Chimpanzees in Uganda's Ruwenzoris, the "Mountains of the Moon," live at altitudes as high as 2,400 feet (750 meters).

There are also subspecies of *Pan troglodytes* living in the same areas of Africa. These chimpanzee populations are becoming increasingly fragmented as humans encroach on their habitats.

ESPECIES Fact Sheets

Chimpanzee -- Kids' Planet -- Defenders of Wildlife - Microsoft Internet Explorer

File Edit View Favorites Tools Help

Address http://www.kidsplanet.org/factsheets/chimpanzee.html   Go

CHIMPANZEE
Pan troglodytes

STATUS:
Endangered

DESCRIPTION:

Like many other animals throughout the world, chimpanzees are an endangered species. Learn about chimps from this Defenders of Wildlife Web site for kids.

Access this Web site from http://www.myreportlinks.com

The western subspecies, known as *Pan troglodytes verus*, can be found in Côte d'Ivoire (formerly Ivory Coast). Small populations of verus can also be found in Guinea-Bissau, Mali, Sierra Leone, Ghana, Senegal, and Liberia. The central subspecies, *Pan troglodytes troglodytes,* are mostly found in Gabon and Cameroon. They can also be found from eastern Nigeria to the Ubanghi River and south to the Zaire River. The eastern subspecies, known as *Pan troglodytes schweinfurthi,* are the chimpanzees studied by Jane Goodall. They inhabit the Democratic Republic of the Congo, Burundi, Rwanda, Uganda, and southern Sudan.

The Gombe Habitat

Jane Goodall studied chimpanzees in Gombe Stream National Park in East Africa. This area is close to the eastern limit of the chimpanzee's range. The park consists of a narrow strip of land, 2 miles (3.2 kilometers) at its widest, that stretches for 10 miles (16 kilometers) along the eastern shore of Lake Tanganyika. The chimp's habitat has been reduced to this tiny space by human encroachment, but that it exists at all is because of Jane Goodall. She was able to convince the Tanzanian government to set this area aside as a national park, and research on chimpanzees continues there forty years later. The lake is a huge body of water, 419.4 miles (675 kilometers) long and 43.5 miles (70 kilometers) wide. It lies at an elevation of 2,542.6 feet (775 meters) above sea level. The Gombe chimpanzee habitat is rugged country where hills rise steeply from the lakeshore to heights of over 4,500 feet (1,400 meters). Steep-sided valleys lie between the hills, and deep ravines cut across the valleys.

Small but Strong

Full-grown chimpanzees are smaller than humans, but they are many times stronger. People who have tried to keep chimps as pets usually learn to their sorrow that this is not a good idea for them or for the chimpanzees. Baby chimps are adorable, and they can be a lot of fun to have around. But by the time they are three years old, chimpanzees are just as strong as an adult human. They have minds of their own and can cause all kinds of mischief. Because they grow even stronger as they get older, they can be very destructive around the house. As a result, owners of chimpanzees often choose to get rid of their pet. The unfortunate chimp usually has to spend the rest of its life in a cage. Since most chimpanzees live about sixty years in captivity, that is a cruel and unjust fate.

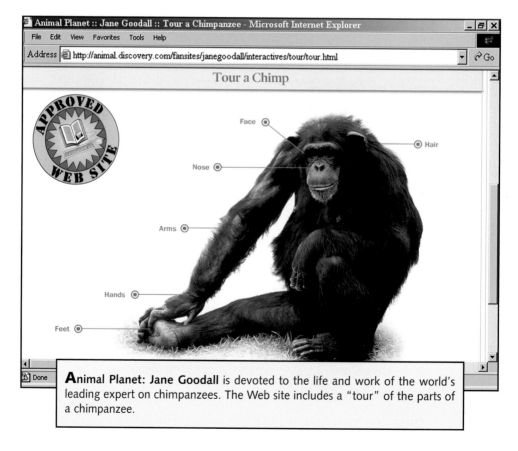

Animal Planet :: Jane Goodall :: Tour a Chimpanzee - Microsoft Internet Explorer

File   Edit   View   Favorites   Tools   Help

Address http://animal.discovery.com/fansites/janegoodall/interactives/tour/tour.html   Go

Tour a Chip

Face

Hair

Nose

Arms

Hands

Feet

Done

Animal Planet: Jane Goodall is devoted to the life and work of the world's leading expert on chimpanzees. The Web site includes a "tour" of the parts of a chimpanzee.

Wild chimpanzees in their native habitat usually live from thirty-five to forty years, rarely reaching the age of fifty.

▶ Physical Characteristics

Full-grown adult male chimpanzees usually weigh from 90 to 115 pounds (41 to 52 kilograms), and are 3 to 4 feet (0.9 to 1.2 meters) tall. Adult female chimps are smaller. They weigh from about 57 to 110 pounds (26 to 50 kilograms) and are 2 to 3.5 feet (0.61 to 1 meter) tall. Chimpanzee arms are very long—longer than their legs. And chimps have a short body. Most of the body is covered with black hair, except on the fingers, palms, armpits, and bottoms of the feet.

The chimpanzee hand is similar to a human hand although a chimp's fingers are longer and its thumb smaller than a human's. Chimps have four fingers and an opposable thumb, so they can easily grasp things. But chimpanzee feet are different from human feet. Chimps can grasp things with their feet, because each foot has five toes including an opposable big toe. Chimpanzees can walk upright as we do. But they usually walk or run along the ground using all fours. They walk on the soles of their feet and use the knuckles of their hands, known as knuckle-walking. Chimps walk upright when they are carrying things in both

Chimpanzees, like humans, are able to express a great deal with their faces.

hands. They sometimes walk upright in order to see over tall grass.

The chimpanzee's face is mostly hairless, although some have a short, white beard. Some adults become bald. Chimps have large ears, small nostrils, and an elongated snout, although their faces are not as elongated as those of other primates. They have a slight brow ridge. Compared to monkeys, chimpanzees have many more muscles in their faces, so they are capable of many expressions. For example, puckered lips indicate the chimp is worried. Chimps will bare their teeth when they are frightened and smile when they are afraid, but they will laugh when they are at play. The chimpanzee sensory systems, including hearing, sight, taste, and touch, are similar to those of humans. Chimps, however, have a much keener sense of smell than humans.

Chapter 3 ▶

CHIMPANZEE BEHAVIOR

Chimpanzees are omnivores—they eat plants and animals. It was long believed that chimpanzees were vegetarians. But in October 1960, during her first year at Gombe, Jane Goodall observed chimpanzees eating meat. She later would see them hunting for meat. Chimps eat small mammals including monkeys and small antelope and have been observed eating birds. Chimpanzees also eat more than twenty types of insects, including termites, ants, and caterpillars, and they have been known to raid beehives to eat the honey.[1] The more than two hundred plant foods in the chimp diet include leaves, fruits, seeds, tree bark, plant bulbs, tender plant shoots, and flowers.

▷ Fishing for Food

Thanks to the pioneering work of Jane Goodall, we now know that chimpanzees use tools, mainly to get food. They often use sticks when eating ants and termites. The sticks allow the chimps to dig into the termites' mounds so that they can

▲ The ability to use objects, such as sticks, as tools sets chimpanzees and other apes apart from most other members of the animal kingdom.

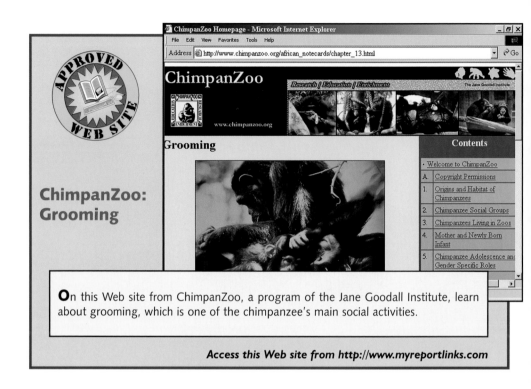

ChimpanZoo:
Grooming

On this Web site from ChimpanZoo, a program of the Jane Goodall Institute, learn about grooming, which is one of the chimpanzee's main social activities.

Access this Web site from http://www.myreportlinks.com

avoid being bitten by termites when they swarm. Chimps have also been observed using stones and wood blocks to crush palm nuts and hard fruits. In November 1960, Goodall first saw chimpanzees "fishing" for termites. She recorded the following observations in her diary:

> *4 November 1960* . . . Saw a black object in front of termite hill. Peered through vegetation. It was a chimp. Quickly dropped down and crawled through the sparse dry grass until I reached a tree with greenery sprouting at the base. Through these leaves could see the chimp about 45 meters away. . . . He turned slightly and, very deliberately, pulled a thick grass stalk toward him and broke off a piece about

45 centimeters long. Then unfortunately, he turned his back on me again. After a few minutes he climbed over the hill and moved away on the far side. I identified him as David Greybeard.

   6 November 1960 By the termite hill were two chimps, both male . . . I could see a little better the use of the piece of straw. It was held in the left hand, poked into the mound, and then removed coated with termites. The straw was raised to the mouth and the insects picked off with the lips along the length of the straw, starting in the middle.[2]

▶ How Chimps Use Tools

Chimpanzees display remarkable intelligence when using tools. They go through a complex process that requires decisions to be made in sequence. According to Goodall, the chimpanzee has an advanced understanding of the relations between things. He can modify objects to make them suitable for a particular purpose. For example, when a chimpanzee arrives at a termite mound to go fishing for termites, he will pick up any suitable nearby material. He may pick up a discarded tool of another chimp who had previously worked the mound. Otherwise, he will look for particular grasses, vines, bark, twigs, or small palm fronds from which to fashion the tool. After carefully checking out clumps of grass or a tangle of vines, the chimp will select a particular length of grass. If he decides that it is not quite the right length, he will discard it immediately and pick another piece.

Chimpanzees use tools made from natural materials to fish for termites, but many grasses and vines used for that purpose must be modified.

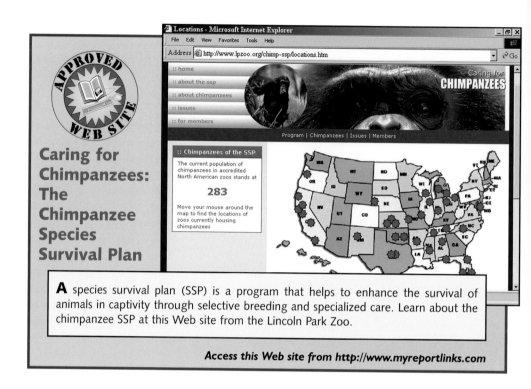

Caring for Chimpanzees: The Chimpanzee Species Survival Plan

A species survival plan (SSP) is a program that helps to enhance the survival of animals in captivity through selective breeding and specialized care. Learn about the chimpanzee SSP at this Web site from the Lincoln Park Zoo.

Access this Web site from http://www.myreportlinks.com

Chimpanzees almost always use tools when fishing for termites. Some materials, such as thin grass or a smooth stem or vine, are suitable as they are. Other materials must be modified before they can be used efficiently. For example, the chimp has to strip leaves from small twigs. Leaflets must be removed from a main leaf rib. And slender fibrous lengths must be stripped from bark, thick stems, or palm fronds. It takes four or five years for a young chimpanzee to learn how to fish for termites using a stick or stem, although young females spend more time watching their mothers and tend to learn these skills more quickly than males, who spend more time playing and developing the social skills they will need as adults.

Other Uses

Chimpanzees also use tools for other purposes. They use sticks and stones as weapons, throwing them at opponents. They have even been observed using a large stick as a club. Chimps also use small sticks to tickle themselves. And they use leaves for a variety of purposes. They use crumpled or chewed-up leaves like a sponge to sop up water to drink. Chimpanzees do not swim, and they do not like to get wet when it rains. Chimps are also concerned with grooming and keeping clean, so they use leaves to carefully wipe themselves after relieving themselves. They also use leaves to dab at bleeding wounds, which they might then lick. And they sometimes use leaves as cushions to keep their bottoms dry when they sit on wet ground. Chimps have also been observed using certain leaves for medicinal purposes.

Chimpanzee groups in different parts of Africa have developed their own unique tool-making traditions. The chimpanzees in Gombe peel the bark from long, straight sticks and use them to pull army ants from their nests. But in the Mahale Mountains, 100 miles (160.9 kilometers) south of Gombe, the chimpanzees do not eat army ants although such ants are readily available. The Mahale chimps use small twigs to take carpenter ants from their nests in tree branches. Carpenter ants are also present in Gombe, but the chimpanzees there do not eat them.

Chimpanzees in West Africa use stones and logs as makeshift hammer-and-anvil tools to open hard-shelled fruits. No East African chimp has been seen using stones in this way, however. Christoph Boesch has studied chimpanzees in the Tai Forest of Côte d'Ivoire, and according to him, it takes a chimpanzee ten years to use a stone as a hammer efficiently. A palm nut has to be hit at just the right angle and hard enough to crack the shell without crushing the nut. "Time and again," writes Boesch, "we have been impressed to see a chimpanzee raise a 20 lb stone above its head, strike a nut with ten or more powerful blows, and then, using the same stone, switch to delicate little taps from a height of only four inches."[3]

▶ Social Habits

Chimpanzees are social animals. They live together in stable groups or communities of about forty to sixty individuals. Some groups have more than one hundred members. Chimpanzee communities are made up of individuals who recognize one another. A chimp can interact peacefully with other members of his own community but will not associate with chimps from other communities.

Chimpanzee mothers spend a great deal of time with their babies. Like their human counterparts, chimp mothers often display a tremendous amount of patience with their precocious offspring.

Each community of chimpanzees has a home range, since communities do not stay within strict boundaries. The size of the home range depends on the type of habitat and the number of chimpanzees in the community. There must be enough food available to support the community and enough chimpanzees to defend their home range from other groups. The average size of the home range varies from about four to twenty square miles (ten to fifty-two square kilometers).

▶ Party Animals

When feeding, chimps also spend time together in smaller groups called parties since the entire community is too big to gather together under most fruit trees. Party membership, however, is constantly changing. Both male and female chimpanzees have almost complete freedom to come and go. A chimpanzee may travel completely alone one day. The next day, he may participate in a small group that is peacefully feeding. Later that day he may be part of a hunting group. Some individual chimpanzees meet with others on a regular basis. Other chimpanzees do not. When parties gather, the chimps need to remember which individuals in their communities make up their party.

Male chimpanzees are more social than females. Males also prefer to socialize with other males with one important exception: when females are in estrus, or ready to mate with a male. Female chimpanzees are very sociable when in estrus. Once a female gives birth, however, she usually spends most of her time with her infant.

All in the Family

Family units consist of a mother and her dependent offspring and often include older offspring. Nursery units consist of two or more family units. Sometimes, these are accompanied by childless females that are not related. All-male parties consist of two or more adult and/or adolescent males. A mixed party consists of one or more adult or adolescent males and one or more adult or adolescent females. The female chimpanzees in such a group may or may not have offspring. A sexual party is a mixed party with one or more of the females in estrus. A party consisting of a male and female chimpanzee in an exclusive relationship is known as a consortship.

A number of factors influence the size and composition of chimpanzee parties from day to day and month to month. When food is scarce, chimpanzees tend to move about in small groups or alone. When food is plentiful, chimpanzees tend to feed together in larger groups. When there are many infants of similar age in the chimpanzee community, mothers often move around

Chimpanzees, like all African apes, often move about on all fours by knuckle-walking.

together. Also, at such times, nursery parties tend to be larger.

Chimpanzees are diurnal, or active during the day. Each evening, chimpanzees build a fresh sleeping nest in the trees. The nests are made of leaves and other plant material. Mother chimpanzees share the nest with their nursing offspring. When they are not nursing, young chimpanzees spend a lot of time playing. Their play activities provide the opportunity to learn survival skills they will need as adults. Through playing, they learn how to use tools, how to make a sleeping nest, how to climb, and how to wrestle.

Behavior Patterns

A social hierarchy exists in each chimpanzee community. In this system, every individual chimp knows his or her place within the group. Relationships can be mostly stable for weeks or months at a time. This is especially true among the older chimpanzees. But changes in relationships are bound to happen and are a normal part of life in the community. As young chimpanzees compete during play, they learn the strengths and weaknesses of their companions. Games become more aggressive as chimps get older. Young males establish themselves as dominant when they challenge first the females and then the senior males of the community. In the community, the dominant male

Chimpanzees use body language and physical contact to communicate with and comfort each other.

is known as the alpha male. Two or more males may form an alliance to compete against others.

Dominance in the community is sometimes established through fights. But often, threats may take the place of actual attacks. Males engage in charging displays in which their hair stands on end. During such displays, they may drag tree branches, wave vegetation around, or beat the ground or trees. A vocal charging display is usually meant as a threat. A silent charging display often precedes an attack.

▶ Cleaning Up

Grooming is the most important daily social activity within the group. Chimpanzees begin learning to groom when they are infants. One purpose of grooming is skin care. By running their fingers gently through their hair, chimps remove dirt and help rid themselves of ticks or lice. But there are other purposes. Social grooming is an important behavior in establishing and maintaining relationships among the chimpanzees. For example, after an episode of aggression in which a chimpanzee has been threatened or attacked, grooming gives reassurance and reduces stress. In this way, grooming serves to restore harmony and maintain friendly relations in the group. It also provides the opportunity for long periods of friendly physical contact. The groomer and the groomed both

This young chimpanzee seems to be deep in thought. Some of those who spend time watching and filming chimps in the wild believe these animals have the capacity to contemplate both animate and inanimate objects.

enjoy the activity as pleasurable and soothing. Grooming also serves as a form of greeting.

Chimpanzees sometimes groom themselves. But usually, grooming sessions involve two or more chimpanzees. Grooming can involve just about any part of the body. Chimpanzees can groom others of the same sex or opposite sex.

▶ The Importance of Body Language

Grooming can be thought of as a type of communication in which information is being exchanged in a physical way. The information involves messages about the emotional state of those involved in the grooming activity. Some scientists have even likened grooming to human gossip. Other common kinds of physical contact include touching, patting, and embracing. These actions convey messages to reassure a chimpanzee who may be distressed. Chimpanzee friends, like human friends, may hold hands, hug, or even kiss. Frightened chimps may hold hands or hug each other.

Body language is important: Chimpanzees use gestures, body postures, and facial expressions as a way of communicating. A hungry chimpanzee will beg for food by approaching others with open hands. Low-ranking chimps greet higher-ups with a posture known as "presenting." The presenting chimp crouches in front of the other chimpanzees, facing away.

Chimpanzees have good memories. They seem to understand that past conflicts need to be resolved before the chimps in a group can get along. Typically, when the loser of a confrontation feels the time is right, he or she approaches the other chimp with an outstretched arm and open hand. This indicates a desire for body contact. The two look into each other's eyes and engage in a long kiss. Another chimp, probably a family member, will embrace the losing chimp.

The various facial expressions convey feelings. Chimpanzees pout in distress and grin in fear or excitement. The full closed grin indicates danger where silence is vital for safety. Lips tightly pressed together indicate readiness to attack. A lip-puckering face indicates worry. And a relaxed face with drooping bottom lip indicates a cheerful and content chimpanzee.

Vocal Communication

According to Jane Goodall, the chimpanzee vocal communication system is quite complex. Chimpanzees have a variety of calls that convey specific emotions or feelings. Sometimes the same call is used for two related emotions, and certain emotions can be conveyed by more than one call. The following list includes the most common types of chimpanzee calls identified by Goodall and other scientists:

Chimpanzee Calls

EMOTION OR FEELING	CALL
Fear (of strangeness)	Wraaa
Puzzlement	Huu
Annoyance	Soft bark (cough)
Social apprehension	Pant-grunt
Social fear	Pant-bark, pant-scream, squeak, victim scream, scream, bark
Anger	Scream, bark, waa-bark, tantrum scream
Rage	Waa-bark, tantrum scream, crying
Distress	Crying, whimper, hoo, SOS scream
Sexual excitement	Copulation scream (squeal), copulation pant
Body-contact enjoyment	Laugh, pant, lip smack, tooth clack
Food enjoyment	Food grunt, food aaa call, pant-hoot, bark, scream
Social excitement	Pant-hoot, bark, scream, roar pant-hoot, arrival pant-hoot
Sociability feelings	Arrival pant-hoot, inquiring pant-hoot, soft grunt, extended grunt, spontaneous pant-hoot, nest grunt[4]

► More About Calls

Chimpanzees use certain calls within a party or small group. These calls include the pant-grunt, whimpering, the hoo, squeaks, screams, barks, laughing, panting, lip smacking, and various grunts.

The pant-grunt is used by a subordinate chimpanzee when communicating with a chimp of higher social rank. This call serves as a token of respect. It helps maintain friendly relations in the chimpanzee community. Whimpers of a distressed chimpanzee can change into screams if the chimpanzee becomes more fearful. Squeaks or short, shrill calls can also change into screams if the chimpanzee's fear increases. High-pitched, loud screams are always given in a series. A chimpanzee being attacked will utter a victim scream. A tantrum scream, a very loud, harsh call, is usually uttered by an infant who has been rejected during weaning, when its mother tries to diminish the time her young nurse. A copulation scream or squeal occurs during mating.

Long sequences of loud, sharp barks are often given during instances of social excitement. Female chimpanzees bark more than males. Chimpanzees laugh when playing, although their laugh is a kind of soft panting done with an open mouth. The play usually involves tickling, play biting, or chasing. Young chimpanzees laugh more than older ones, because they do more playing.

A chimpanzee brachiating, or swinging from branch to branch. By using their long arms to move from tree to tree in the forest, chimps can reach fruit on thin branches that would not normally support their weight.

But older chimpanzees sometimes laugh while playing with young chimps or even with other adult chimps.

Long-Distance Calls

Chimpanzees use certain distance calls to relay information to one or more individuals who are not part of the caller's immediate group. Some calls serve to call attention to rich sources of food or danger in the environment. Other calls announce the location of specific group members so that vocal contact can be maintained. Yet other calls are cries for help.

The pant-hoots of adult chimpanzees identify the caller. Each chimpanzee's pant-hoot is unique. Chimpanzees give what is called an arrival pant-hoot when they find a food source or join another party. When a male chimpanzee arrives on a high ridge during travel, he will give the inquiring pant-hoot. This is often accompanied by drumming on a tree. The chimpanzee leaps up and pounds his hands and feet against the tree. The sound can carry for long distances.

The SOS scream, a loud, high-pitched call for help, is made by a chimpanzee who has been attacked or is about to be attacked. Crying, another type of call for help, is uttered by a young chimpanzee in distress. Often this occurs when the chimpanzee has been temporarily separated from its

During a male chimpanzee's courtship display, he may gaze intently at the female.

mother. The crying consists of tantrum screaming and loud whimpering. It is heard by the mother, who then rushes to rejoin her offspring.

Reproduction

By the time they reach twelve or thirteen years of age, chimpanzees are fully grown and are able to reproduce. Female chimpanzees become sexually active around the age of ten as adult males become interested in them. By age thirteen or fourteen, females can become pregnant during a cycle that lasts on average thirty-five days. During the cycle, the female chimpanzee's sex organs become swollen and pink, giving a visual clue to the males that the female is in estrus, ready for mating. The larger the swelling, the more likely the female is to conceive. Males will be most attracted to such females, and their mating behavior will include grooming the female as well as fighting off other males that come close to her.

Before mating can take place, the male chimpanzee engages in a courtship display to attract the attention of the female. The courtship may include shaking a branch, stretching out one or both arms to the female, rocking from side to side, swaggering on two feet, stamping with one foot, or hitting the ground with the knuckles of one hand. He may also gaze intently at the female.

Young chimpanzees sleep in a nest with their mother until they stop nursing, but they are not ready for independence until they are seven years old or so.

Usually, female chimps mate with all the males in a community, which gives each male a chance to father her young. That way, the males will be more likely to treat the offspring well. When the female is at her most fertile, though, the most-aggressive and highest-ranking males stay close to her, preventing other males from mating with her. Occasionally, a male chimpanzee succeeds in forming an exclusive relationship with a female, in a relationship called a consortship. The male leads the female away from the group, away from the attentions of competing males. The consortship can last from several days to two weeks or longer. Female chimps, though, do not form a bond with one male for life.

▶ Baby Chimps

Chimpanzee pregnancy lasts about eight months. A chimpanzee usually gives birth to a single baby. Chimpanzee twins are extremely rare, and when they do occur, it is very difficult for the mother to take care of both, since the young chimps are totally dependent on their mothers. Chimpanzee mothers take very good care of their babies. They have learned what to do from watching their own mothers. They provide the baby with warmth, nourishment, transportation, and protection. Chimpanzees nurse for five years. By the time they are six months old, the baby chimp can

▲ *A baby chimpanzee nurses from its mother. The bond between infant and mother is a strong one and often lasts well beyond adolescence.*

ride on its mother's back by grasping the fur. Each night the young chimpanzee sleeps with its mother in a nest in the trees. After the young chimpanzee is weaned, it builds its own nest in the trees.

At age seven, most chimpanzees are ready to begin their own lives, no longer needing to stay with their mothers. Chimpanzees are adults by the age of thirteen. But even as adults, chimpanzees often remain close to their mothers for many years.

EARLY RESEARCH

When chimpanzees were first brought to Europe, people who saw them were amazed. The creatures seemed so similar to humans, like tiny people. Yet they were clearly not people—only half human, half beast. The first chimpanzee arrived in Europe in 1630. It was brought from Angola and given as a gift to the Prince of Orange in the Netherlands. Several more chimpanzees arrived in Europe over the next few decades. They were kept in zoos for the entertainment of visitors. In 1661, Samuel Pepys, an Englishman most famous for his diary of British life in the 1660s, came across a chimpanzee. He was impressed by the creature's intelligence, and wrote that it "might be taught to speak or make signs."[1]

▷ Different Views of Chimpanzees

Scientists in Europe were fascinated but did not know what to make of these strange creatures. Aristotle, the ancient Greek philosopher, had spoken about apes more than two thousand years

▲ When chimpanzees were first brought to the Western world's attention, they were often treated as an attraction for how much like humans they seemed—or could be made to appear. Here, a chimpanzee at the National Zoo in Washington, D.C., in 1926 is posed at a table with a glass of milk.

ago. But people had long since believed them to be creatures of mythology.

Africans, however, had a very different view of chimpanzees. The various peoples of West Africa had lived with chimpanzees for thousands of years. Some saw the apes as almost human, some as fully human. Africans were aware that chimpanzees use stone tools, organize activities such as hunting, and medicate themselves with native plants. To the Oubi people of Côte d'Ivoire, chimpanzees are "ugly human beings." The Oubi believe chimpanzees are spiritually superior to humans and should not be hunted. The Mende people of the Upper Guinean forests call chimpanzees "different persons." They believe chimpanzees and humans have a common ancestor. One group of Gouro people believe they are descendants of chimpanzees. To the Baoulé people, the chimpanzee is the "beloved brother" of man. The Bakwé people, thinking of chimpanzees as close relatives, buried them as men. And the Bété people call the chimpanzee the "wild man" or "man returned to the forest."[2]

▶ European Views

Meanwhile, back in Europe, men of science called chimpanzees "pygmies." In 1699, Edward Tyson, a London physician, dissected a chimpanzee to compare the anatomy of a "pygmy" and a human

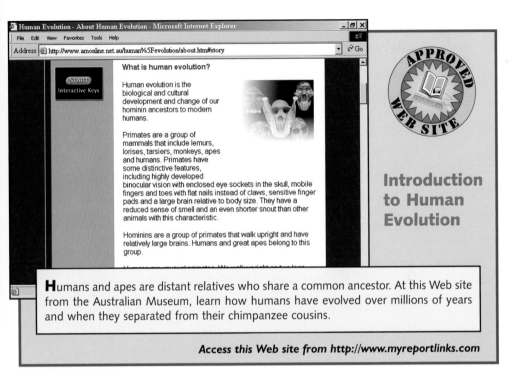

What is human evolution?

Human evolution is the biological and cultural development and change of our hominin ancestors to modern humans.

Primates are a group of mammals that include lemurs, lorises, tarsiers, monkeys, apes and humans. Primates have some distinctive features, including highly developed binocular vision with enclosed eye sockets in the skull, mobile fingers and toes with flat nails instead of claws, sensitive finger pads and a large brain relative to body size. They have a reduced sense of smell and an even shorter snout than other animals with this characteristic.

Hominins are a group of primates that walk upright and have relatively large brains. Humans and great apes belong to this group.

Introduction to Human Evolution

Humans and apes are distant relatives who share a common ancestor. At this Web site from the Australian Museum, learn how humans have evolved over millions of years and when they separated from their chimpanzee cousins.

Access this Web site from http://www.myreportlinks.com

being. He found many similarities. According to Tyson, this "Creature so very remarkable . . . [was] . . . a sort of *Animal* so much resembling *Man,* that both the Ancients and the Moderns have reputed it to be a *Puny Race* of Mankind."[3]

C. E. Hoppius, in 1789, was particularly interested in the ways in which chimpanzees resembled humans. He pointed to similarities in body structure, including face, ears, mouth, teeth, hands, and breasts. He also mentioned similarities in food, imitation, and gestures. Hoppius was inspired to write the following: "Since therefore no one, without extraordinary delight and wonder, can look upon the living genus of Simiae [the group of related species to which chimpanzees belong], so utterly ridiculous and curious, those just mentioned, which are most like men, should be studied with open minds by experts in natural history."[4]

The Influence of Charles Darwin

In 1860, Charles Darwin's just-published theory of evolution, *The Origin of Species,* set off a firestorm of controversy. In that groundbreaking work, Darwin wrote that humans had evolved from apes. Many, especially those who took the biblical view of our human origin literally, were outraged at the idea that human beings could be descended from apes. Caricatures of Darwin showing him as half human and half ape appeared on newspaper editorial pages. Some scientists, though, including the naturalist Thomas Huxley, came out in support of Darwin. In 1863, Huxley argued that anatomical evidence showed that humans are related to apes through a common ancestor.

Amid the controversy, Darwin continued his research and writing. His book *The Descent of Man* was published in 1871. In it, Darwin concluded that humans are descended from an apelike creature. He theorized that apes had the ability to reason, to use tools, to imitate, and to remember, writing, "There is no fundamental difference between man and the higher mammals in the mental faculties."[5] In *The Expression of the Emotions in Man and Animals,*

When Charles Darwin proposed in 1860 that humans were descended from an apelike ancestor, his theories were met with outrage by many, especially those who took the biblical story of creation literally.

Memoir Wolgang Koehler - Microsoft Internet Explorer

File Edit View Favorites Tools Help

Address http://wkprc.eva.mpg.de/english/files/wolfgang_koehler.htm   Go

MPI - Department
of Psychology

Home

Wolfgang Köhler

Facilities

Ape List

New! Enrichment
for apes

Projects

Publications

■ German Page

Memoir Wolfgang Köhler

(Text: K. Jensen)

"We wished to ascertain the degree of relationship between anthropoid apes and man in a field which seems to us particularly important, but on which we have as yet little information." (Köhler, 1925, p. 1)

The work for which Wolfgang Köhler is most likely to be remembered, and for which the Primate Research Centre is a tribute, was on the mental abilities of apes.

Köhler was born in Reval, Estonia on January 21, 1887. His family moved to Germany when he was six years old, and he was raised in Wolfenbüttel. Köhler attended university in Tübingen, Bonn as well as Berlin. In Berlin, he did his PhD research on psycho-acoustics, and studied under the likes of Max Planck (physics) and Karl Stumpf (psychology).

After completing his PhD, Köhler worked at the Psychological Institute in Frankfurt-am-Main, where he met Max Wertheimer and Kurt Koffka. Together, they formed a new branch of psychology called Gestalt. They opposed the structuralist view

The Web site for the **Wolfgang Köhler Primate Research Center** in Leipzig, Germany, contains this brief biographical sketch of the psychologist who conducted research into the intelligence of chimpanzees.

EDITOR'S CHOICE

published in 1873, Darwin argued that the complex behavior as well as the complex anatomy of human beings evolved from apelike ancestors.

Those who accepted Darwin's ideas began to focus on the behavior of chimpanzees. Some exaggerated the similarities between humans and apes. They also tended to overestimate the intelligence and abilities of apes. After all, if humans were truly descended from the apes, then it seemed only natural to view apes in the image of humans. Victor Meunier, a Frenchman, even proposed that chimpanzees be trained as domestic servants, seeing them capable of serving food. According to Meunier, they could also work as gardeners, nursemaids, valets, chambermaids, construction workers, factory workers, and so forth. These fanciful ideas of Meunier and others were not, of course, based on any scientific evidence. A scientific approach to studying the chimpanzee would not happen until the next century.

Wolfgang Köhler: Studying the Mind of the Chimpanzee

Serious scientific studies of chimpanzee behavior began in the early part of the twentieth century. The first major scientist to turn his attention to chimpanzees was the German psychologist Wolfgang Köhler. He was interested in learning more about the mental processes of human beings. He was familiar with the ideas of Charles Darwin. And he was particularly drawn to Darwin's notion that humans are part of the continuity of life. So with that in mind, Köhler decided to conduct psychological studies of chimpanzees. In this way, he hoped to learn just how the thought processes of humans and chimpanzees were similar and how they were different.

In 1913, Köhler became director of the newly established Anthropoid Station of the Prussian Academy of Science in Tenerife in the Canary Islands. For the next five years, he studied nine captive chimpanzees. Köhler tested the chimpanzees in various situations that required them to solve a particular problem. Often, this involved the use of tools to get food. For example, he would suspend a banana out of the reach of the chimps. In order to get the banana, the chimps had to stack boxes together and climb up. Another test involved having to insert a narrow stick into a thicker one to produce a tool long enough to reach the food. In this situation, it took the chimpanzee, named Sultan, an hour to figure out how to join the sticks. Once he accomplished that, however, he immediately reached the food.

Insightful Apes

To Köhler, these experiments proved that chimpanzees had insight. They could solve a problem based upon their perception of the relationships between things. Sometimes they could solve a problem even when something necessary was not present. Sultan once was unable to reach a suspended treat. He paused, remaining motionless. Then he ran off to get a box that he had passed earlier that day in another room. He returned with the box and used it to get the reward. Sometimes chimpanzees solved new problems by watching and imitating the behavior of others.

Köhler wrote about his work with the chimpanzees in *The Mentality of Apes,* published in

1925. He said that chimpanzees demonstrate intelligent behavior of the general kind familiar in human beings. However, Köhler concluded that "Even assuming the anthropoid ape behaves intelligently in the sense in which the word is applied to man, there is yet from the very start no doubt that he remains in this respect far behind man, becoming perplexed and making mistakes in relatively simple situations; but it is precisely for this reason that we may, under the simplest conditions, gain knowledge of the nature of intelligent acts."[6]

Empathetic Apes

While Köhler was gaining knowledge about chimpanzees, a young psychologist in Russia named Nadezhda Ladygina-Kohts, also known as Nadia Kohts, was carrying out her own research into primate behavior. In 1916, she brought a year-and-a-half-old male chimpanzee into her home in Moscow. For the next four years, she raised Joni, the chimp, as if he were her own child. She gave Joni hundreds of problem-solving tests. Later, when she had her own son, she gave him similar tests during the first four years of his life. She compared their behaviors and expressions of emotion and found similarities. One of her most interesting observations had to do with arousing sympathy in Joni. She found that the only way she could coax the chimp off the roof of her home was

Two young chimps embrace in a show of affection. Scientists suggest that chimpanzees are not just emotionally connected to each other for their own sake but for the sake of the other chimpanzee as well.

to pretend that she was upset. Joni responded by trying to make Nadia feel better.

> If I pretend to be crying, close my eyes and weep, Joni immediately stops his plays or any other activities, quickly runs over to me, all excited and shagged, from the most remote places . . . from where I could not drive him down despite my persistent calls and entreaties. He hastily runs around me, as if looking for the offender; looking at my face, he tenderly takes my chin in his palm, lightly touches my face with his finger, as though trying to understand what is happening, and turns around, clenching his toes into firm fists.[7]

Dr. Frans de Waal, a leading primatologist, suggests that such behavior indicates apes are more than just emotionally connected to others—that they can actually appreciate the situations of others.[8]

▶ Robert M. Yerkes: Raising and Observing Chimpanzees

Another early pioneer of chimpanzee behavioral research was the psychologist Robert Yerkes. Like Köhler, Yerkes was influenced by the ideas of Charles Darwin. Yerkes had long been interested in the thinking and behavior of apes because of their closeness to human beings. He believed that learning more about apes could lead to greater understanding of the roots of human behavior. In 1916, Yerkes called for the establishment of a primate research institute.

In the early 1920s, Yerkes spent some time observing captive chimpanzees in Cuba. He made up his mind to raise chimps on his own so that he could conduct research.

Research Moves On

Yerkes bought two chimps, Chim and Panzee, from a zoo. For a while, the chimpanzees lived in a bedroom in Yerkes' home. Yerkes wrote about the summer he spent with the chimps in his book *Almost Human,* published in 1924. That year, Yerkes began teaching at Yale University, where he founded the Yale Laboratories of Primate Biology. His two chimps became the center of a chimpanzee colony.

In 1930, Yerkes moved his laboratory to Orange Park, Florida. That year, a chimpanzee was born at the laboratory. Yerkes was able to observe in great detail the chimpanzee's growth, development, and reproductive process.

Yerkes and his colleagues were learning a great deal about chimpanzee behavior in the laboratory, but Yerkes also wanted to learn about the behavior of chimpanzees in their native habitat. So he sent Henry Nissen from the laboratory to observe chimpanzees in French Guinea. Nissen spent two and a half months in Africa. World War II, however, brought about a slowdown in the research on chimpanzee behavior. The next big leap forward in research on chimpanzees would not take place until 1960, when Jane Goodall arrived in Africa.

Chapter 5

JANE GOODALL AND THE CHIMPANZEES OF GOMBE

Jane Goodall is the person most people associate with the chimpanzee. She spent many years observing and studying chimpanzees in their native African habitat. As the world's foremost authority on chimpanzees, she has contributed greatly to our understanding of our closest relative. However, she was not the only person who wanted to learn more about the chimpanzees in Africa. At around the time of Goodall's arrival in East Africa in July 1960, others had already begun their research.

▶ Renewed Interest in the Chimpanzee

In early 1960, animal behaviorist Adriaan Kortlandt from the Netherlands began a short field study of chimpanzees in the eastern Belgian Congo (which became known as Zaire and is now the Democratic Republic of the Congo). He noticed a dramatic difference between these wild chimpanzees and the captive chimps he had seen in zoos. The chimpanzees in Africa seemed more lively and more interested in everything. Indeed, they seemed almost human. Kortlandt felt as if he was "looking at some strange kind of human beings dressed in furs. . . . Once I saw a chimpanzee gaze at a particularly beautiful sunset for a full 15 minutes."[1]

Also in 1960, Junichiro Itani from Japan carried out brief field studies of chimpanzees in the Mahale Mountains south of Kigoma, Tanzania. This would later lead to longer-term studies. Kortlandt returned to Africa to study chimpanzees in Guinea in 1968. Other scientists carried out field research in Uganda, Senegal, Gabon, and the Ivory Coast, now Côte d'Ivoire.

Scientists approached their observations and studies from different angles. While some ventured into the tropical forests of Africa, others brought chimpanzees into their homes. Some worked with chimpanzees in trailers, while others studied the apes in enclosures. Some researchers even took captive chimpanzees and reintroduced them into the African jungle.

▶ Jane Goodall's Early Years at Gombe

Jane Goodall arrived in Gombe, in Tanganyika, in July 1960. (Tanganyika and Zanzibar united to form Tanzania in 1964.) Goodall would spend most of the next three decades there, living among the area's wild chimpanzees. Jane Goodall had been sent to Africa by Louis Leakey, the famous

Photograph by Hugo Van Lawick, courtesy of the Jane Goodall Institute.

▲ Flint with the young researcher Jane Goodall. This baby chimp was the first
wild infant whose development Goodall was able to study in any detail.

anthropologist. Leakey believed that the human species, *Homo sapiens,* had originated in Africa. He and his wife, Mary, had been digging for fossils at Olduvai Gorge and other places in East Africa. They had uncovered thousands of fossilized bones and skull fragments that came from the ancestors of modern humans. They also found tens of thousands of ancient stone tools.

Leakey believed that studies of the great apes, humankind's closest relatives, would lead to more information about how early humans lived. So with that in mind, Leakey sent three women into the field to study the great apes. He sent Dian Fossey to study the mountain gorillas of Rwanda and Zaire. He sent Biruté Galdikas to study the orangutans of Borneo. And he sent Jane Goodall to study the chimpanzees of Gombe. He chose women because he believed that they would be less threatening to the male-dominated ape communities.

▷ From Secretary to Scientist

Goodall had worked for Leakey as his secretary during her visit to Kenya in 1957 and 1958. Leakey decided that she would be a perfect choice. She was an exceptionally intelligent and energetic woman and was fascinated with animals and nature. At the time, Leakey considered it a plus that Goodall lacked formal scientific training. He felt that this

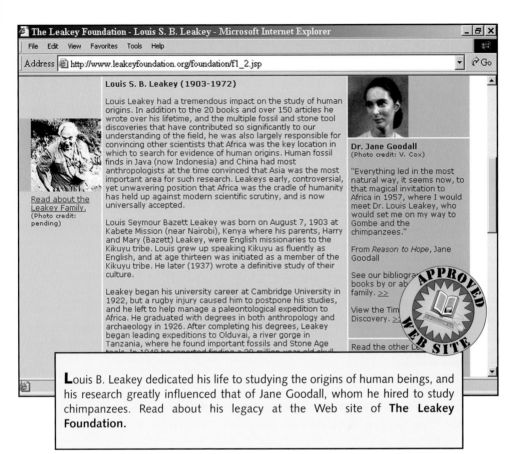

Louis S. B. Leakey (1903-1972)

Louis Leakey had a tremendous impact on the study of human origins. In addition to the 20 books and over 150 articles he wrote over his lifetime, and the multiple fossil and stone tool discoveries that have contributed so significantly to our understanding of the field, he was also largely responsible for convincing other scientists that Africa was the key location in which to search for evidence of human origins. Human fossil finds in Java (now Indonesia) and China had most anthropologists at the time convinced that Asia was the most important area for such research. Leakeys early, controversial, yet unwavering position that Africa was the cradle of humanity has held up against modern scientific scrutiny, and is now universally accepted.

Louis Seymour Bazett Leakey was born on August 7, 1903 at Kabete Mission (near Nairobi), Kenya where his parents, Harry and Mary (Bazett) Leakey, were English missionaries to the Kikuyu tribe. Louis grew up speaking Kikuyu as fluently as English, and at age thirteen was initiated as a member of the Kikuyu tribe. He later (1937) wrote a definitive study of their culture.

Leakey began his university career at Cambridge University in 1922, but a rugby injury caused him to postpone his studies, and he left to help manage a paleontological expedition to Africa. He graduated with degrees in both anthropology and archaeology in 1926. After completing his degrees, Leakey began leading expeditions to Olduvai, a river gorge in Tanzania, where he found important fossils and Stone Age

Read about the
Leakey Family.
(Photo credit:
pending)

Dr. Jane Goodall
(Photo credit: V. Cox)

"Everything led in the most natural way, it seems now, to that magical invitation to Africa in 1957, where I would meet Dr. Louis Leakey, who would set me on my way to Gombe and the chimpanzees."

From *Reason to Hope*, Jane Goodall

See our bibliogra books by or ab family. >>

View the Tim Discovery. >

Read the other L

Louis B. Leakey dedicated his life to studying the origins of human beings, and his research greatly influenced that of Jane Goodall, whom he hired to study chimpanzees. Read about his legacy at the Web site of **The Leakey Foundation.**

way, she would approach her chimpanzee research with an open mind. So he sent Goodall to Gombe because he knew that chimpanzees lived there in a protected area of forest on the eastern edge of Lake Tanganyika. In 1961, Leakey was so impressed with the progress Goodall had made that he decided scientific education would now be valuable. He arranged for Goodall to return to England to study at the University of Cambridge. For the next three years, she divided her time between Cambridge and Gombe. In 1964, she earned a doctorate in ethology, the scientific study of animal behavior.

Goodall's First Contact With the Chimpanzees

Goodall arrived at Gombe on July 16, 1960. Her mother, Vanne, accompanied her and spent the first three months with her. Before the trip to Gombe, Goodall had read every book or research paper on chimpanzees she could get her hands on. Practically all of the material dealt with chimpanzees in captivity. Very little field research, or study of chimps in their natural habitat, had been done yet.

On her first day in Gombe, Goodall walked into the forest and climbed up on a high ridge. From there she could see down into the valley. She encountered a troop of baboons and various small animals on her walk, but she saw no chimpanzees. The next day, Goodall went into the forest again, and this time she saw two chimpanzees feeding in a tree. But as soon as they saw her, they climbed down and silently disappeared into the forest. Each day after that, Goodall went searching for chimpanzees but came across none. Finally, when a week had gone by, she spotted chimpanzees on the other side of the valley, feeding.

Goodall set out at 5:30 each morning, hoping to get closer to the chimpanzees without scaring

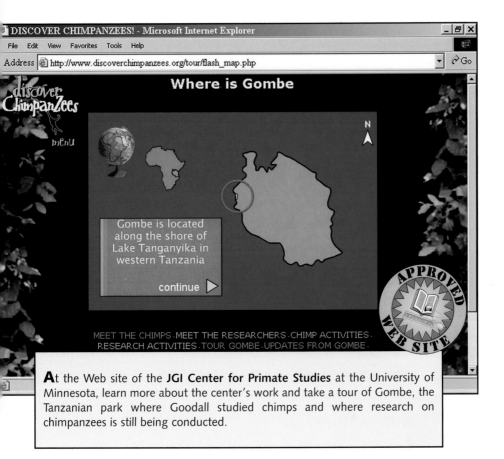

DISCOVER CHIMPANZEES! - Microsoft Internet Explorer

File   Edit   View   Favorites   Tools   Help

Address http://www.discoverchimpanzees.org/tour/flash_map.php

Where is Gombe

Gombe is located along the shore of Lake Tanganyika in western Tanzania

continue ▷

N

MEET THE CHIMPS · MEET THE RESEARCHERS · CHIMP ACTIVITIES · RESEARCH ACTIVITIES · TOUR GOMBE · UPDATES FROM GOMBE ·

At the Web site of the **JGI Center for Primate Studies** at the University of Minnesota, learn more about the center's work and take a tour of Gombe, the Tanzanian park where Goodall studied chimps and where research on chimpanzees is still being conducted.

them away. But the chimpanzees proved to be very shy. Whenever they saw Goodall, they moved away. One day, she discovered a hill that would provide a good vantage point for watching the chimpanzees. She called the hill "the Peak." This became her favorite viewing spot. She spent many hours sitting there patiently with her binoculars. She watched the chimpanzees whenever they came into view. Eventually the chimpanzees became used to this strange creature with the binoculars.

By October 1960, Goodall was able to move in closer to the chimpanzees without them running away. By this point, she had begun to recognize individual chimpanzees. She gave them names so that she could keep track of them. Little by little, Goodall began to learn how the chimpanzees lived, watching them form small groups within a community. On October 30, she made a startling discovery when she observed some chimpanzees eating meat. Up till then, it was believed that chimpanzees were vegetarians. Then on November 4, 1960, Goodall made another important discovery: She observed two chimpanzees, David Greybeard and Goliath, making tools to take termites from their mounds.

A Breakthrough

Around this time, David Greybeard had begun venturing into Goodall's camp. At first, he fed on the ripe red fruits growing on the oil-nut palm. Then he took some bananas that he found in the camp. One day, David Greybeard came up to Goodall in the camp and took the banana that she offered him. Later, he would come up to Goodall when he saw her in the forest, looking to see if she had a banana for him. This was a major breakthrough for Goodall. Now that the other chimps saw that David Greybeard was not afraid, they realized that Goodall was not a threat to them.

Eventually other chimpanzees began visiting Goodall's camp—Goliath, William, old Flo and her family, and others. From then on, Goodall was able to move among the chimpanzees and carry out her research at close range. Over the years at Gombe, Goodall gradually built a team to help with the research.

▶ Chimpanzee Aggression

In his 1963 book *On Aggression,* Konrad Lorenz, the so-called father of ethology, wrote that human beings are the only mammals who kill members of their own species. Now, thanks to the work of Jane Goodall and other researchers, we know better. But such violence among animals is not an every-day occurrence.

Typically, chimpanzees will threaten an opponent into submission rather than actually attack. A dominant alpha male will charge another male chimpanzee who tries to challenge his authority. The alpha male displays anger and strength as he rushes at his rival. He screams as he hurtles through the brush, slapping tree trunks and the ground. If the challenger stands his ground, a fight will occur. Such a fight can be violent, even deadly. When a chimpanzee attacks another, he usually jumps on the victim's back. He will bite his victim, pull his hair, and may drag or slam him to the ground.

Chimpanzees are territorial. One of the roles of male chimpanzees is maintaining, defending, or enlarging the home range of the community. Small groups of male chimps routinely patrol the borders of their range. The group members work as a team in keeping invaders out of their range. Sometimes, a neighboring community itself will be attacked. Territorial disputes between chimpanzee communities sometimes result in an ongoing state of war that can last a surprisingly long time.

▶ Hostilities Emerge

In 1972, Goodall witnessed the breakup of the community into two separate groups. This was caused by a dispute between aspiring alpha male chimps and their supporters. A chimp named Humphrey led the northern group. This included Humphrey's followers Evered, Faben, Figan, Hugo, Jomeo, Mike, and Satan. The group led by Hugh and Charlie claimed the southern part of the range as their territory. This group included De, Gode, Willy Wally, and Goliath.

By the next year, Goodall observed that there was no longer any friendly interaction between members of the northern and southern groups. Chance encounters between teams patrolling the borders of their territories were increasingly hostile. The two groups were now enemies. By 1974, a state of war existed between the two groups.

Animal Diversity Web: *Pan troglodytes* (chimpanzee)

On this Web site from the University of Michigan's Museum of Zoology, you will find detailed information on the chimpanzee.

Access this Web site from http://www.myreportlinks.com

The war would last for four years! And during this time, Goodall was deeply shocked by the violence she witnessed.

Chimpanzees have a very strong sense of group identity. They know who belongs to their community and who does not. If outsiders are detected near the community's home range, they are often attacked so aggressively that they die from their wounds. Groups of males will also patrol their community's borders to keep outsiders from entering and will only take on an intruder when they have the advantage in number. At Gombe, Humphrey's northern group carried out systematic, planned attacks on the southern group. Besides

International Primate Protection League ~ IPPL ~ Working To Protect All Living Primates Since 1 - Micr...

File   Edit   View   Favorites   Tools   Help

Address http://www.ippl.org/about.html   Go

IPPL

About Us
Our Sanctuary
Alerts
News & Archives
Become A Member
On-Line Catalog
Multimedia
Related Links
Contact Us

International Primate Protection League

© Tilo Nadler

Royal praise for deserving

About Us

The International Primate Protection League was founded in 1973, and, since this time, has been working continuously for the well-being of primates. IPPL has Field Representatives in 31 countries. Its Advisory Board is composed of experts from the fields of zoology, anthropology, medicine, biology, veterinary medicine, and psychology. Many IPPL officers have lived for long periods with primates in their natural habitats.

Primates are disappearing at an alarming rate. Every primate species is listed on the appendices of the Convention on International Trade in Endangered Species. All apes, (gorillas, orangutans, chimpanzees, bonobos, and gibbons), all lemurs, and many monkeys appear on the Convention's Appendix 1, the list reserved for the most endangered species. All other primates are listed on Appendix II.

In countries where primates live, IPPL's Field Representatives work to create and preserve national parks and sanctuaries, and for bans on primate hunting, trapping,

The International Primate Protection League, made up of experts in zoology, anthropology, medicine, biology, veterinary medicine, and psychology, works to safeguard the world's primate species. Learn more about the organization's efforts from its Web site.

Access this Web site from http://www.myreportlinks.com

killing their male rivals, they also killed females, infants, and the elderly.

In 1975, Goodall was especially shocked to learn that chimpanzees are also capable of cannibalism. Passion and Pom, a mother and daughter team, attacked female chimpanzees in their own community, stole their babies, and then killed and ate the babies. As for the war, it finally ended when the last of the southern group males was killed. The victorious northern group took up residence in their newly won southern territory. But soon, a powerful chimpanzee community to their south began venturing north. Humphrey's group eventually had to retreat northward.

The events of 1974 to 1978 caused Goodall to change her view of chimps. Up until then, she had believed that while chimpanzees could be violent on occasion, they were still "nicer" than human beings. Now Goodall knew that chimpanzees are capable of premeditated warfare. And she felt that they are even more like human beings than she had thought.

Thinking of Others

Occasional episodes of such violence among chimpanzees are shocking, but peaceful behavior is more typical than aggressive behavior. Threats occur much more often than actual fights. And brief, relatively mild fights happen more often than vicious attacks resulting in wounds or death. Those who have spent time observing chimpanzees in the wild or working with them in captivity have learned that chimps are able to see things from another individual's perspective. This ability, which chimpanzees share with humans, allows them to feel for others. And this in turn often leads to acts of altruism, behavior that benefits another.

Many acts of altruistic behavior by chimpanzees have been observed by researchers. Jane Goodall learned that a chimpanzee mother will risk severe punishment to save her child. In one instance, she saw a chimpanzee called Melissa leap at Mike, an alpha male, as he dragged her

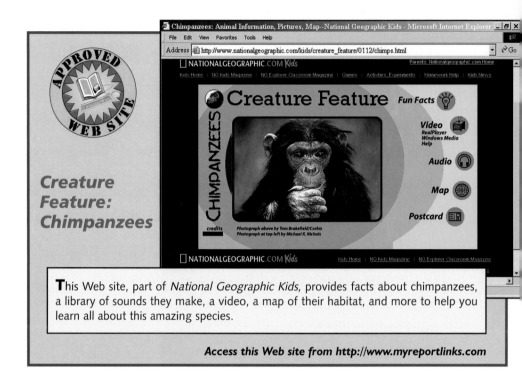

Creature Feature: Chimpanzees

This Web site, part of *National Geographic Kids,* provides facts about chimpanzees, a library of sounds they make, a video, a map of their habitat, and more to help you learn all about this amazing species.

Access this Web site from http://www.myreportlinks.com

child. Mike dropped the child and attacked Melissa. Often, an infant or young chimpanzee will try to help its mother if she is being attacked.

One day, Goodall saw a young female chimpanzee rescue her infant brother. The two chimps were walking through the forest when they came across a large snake. Pom, the sister, quickly climbed up a tree. Prof, the infant, kept walking right toward the snake. Most likely he did not see it. Pom, seeing that her brother was in danger, leaped down from the safety of the tree. She pulled Prof into her arms and carried him safely back up the tree.

There are also instances of chimpanzees taking risks for other chimps they are not even close to. One of the most dramatic examples involved Washoe, a female chimpanzee who became famous when she learned to communicate with humans using American Sign Language. When Washoe was nine, she lived at a captive chimpanzee colony in Norman, Oklahoma. Like other similar colonies, this colony was situated on human-made islands surrounded by water-filled moats. The chimpanzees could not escape because they cannot swim and were afraid to go in the water. One day, a three-year-old female chimpanzee called Cindy fell into the moat. She splashed wildly

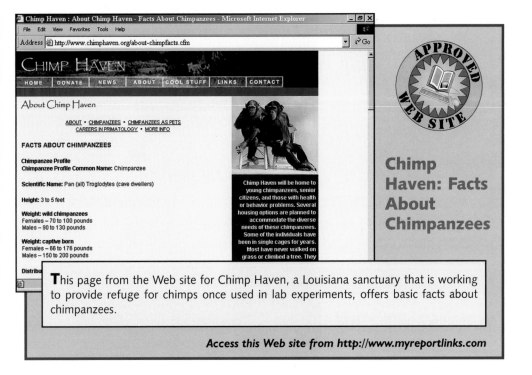

This page from the Web site for Chimp Haven, a Louisiana sanctuary that is working to provide refuge for chimps once used in lab experiments, offers basic facts about chimpanzees.

Access this Web site from http://www.myreportlinks.com

Among primates, chimpanzees have hands that most resemble ours.

and was in danger of drowning. Seeing what had happened, Washoe clung to a clump of grass and stepped into the water. She grabbed Cindy's arm and pulled her to safety. Washoe was not related to Cindy but risked her life to save her anyway. In a similar situation at Lion Country Safari in Florida, a male chimpanzee drowned while attempting to rescue an infant chimp.

Sharing Meals

Mothers usually share food with their offspring. Sharing of food among adult chimpanzees depends on the type of food. While adults almost always share meat, they rarely share plant foods. Interestingly, adult female chimpanzees hardly ever share with each other. But adult males often share with other males and with females. If a male chimp has captured a monkey, other chimps gather around and beg for a piece. They will even sometimes put their hands into the other chimp's mouth to try to take food from it. Humans see sharing as a kind behavior, but for chimpanzees, it may just mean that it is easier to give up a small piece of food than to be bothered by another chimp while eating.

Chimpanzees in captivity have also been observed sharing their food. Köhler, in *The Mentality of Apes,* wrote about how one chimpanzee, in response to another chimp's begging,

The social interactions among chimpanzees sometimes even extend to sharing food.

"may suddenly gather some fruit together and hold it out to the other or take the banana which he was just going to put in his mouth, break it in half and hand one piece to the other."[2] Similar food sharing in response to begging has been observed by many researchers.

▷ Caring for the Ill

Another altruistic behavior among chimpanzees involves caring for the sick. At Gombe, Jane Goodall observed family members caring for their sick but not for unrelated chimpanzees. When Fifi showed up with a gash in her head, the other chimps moved away in fear. But caring for the sick between unrelated chimpanzees is quite common among captive chimps. Köhler and others observed chimps removing splinters from others and squeezing pus from wounds. W. R. Miles observed an adult male chimpanzee removing a speck of dirt from his companion's eye in response to her whimpering. Another researcher saw a chimpanzee groom her companion's teeth and take out a molar that was loose. Chimpanzees often show that they understand the needs or wants of an individual who is suffering. Their ability to empathize enables chimpanzees to feel compassion for others, which makes them a rare species indeed—and a species that it is important to protect.

CHIMPANZEE-HUMAN COMMUNICATION

Robert Yerkes was impressed with how smart the chimpanzees he studied were. They had an amazing ability to imitate his actions. Although these chimps never imitated sounds, he theorized that they could understand from one hundred to two hundred words of spoken English. Yerkes

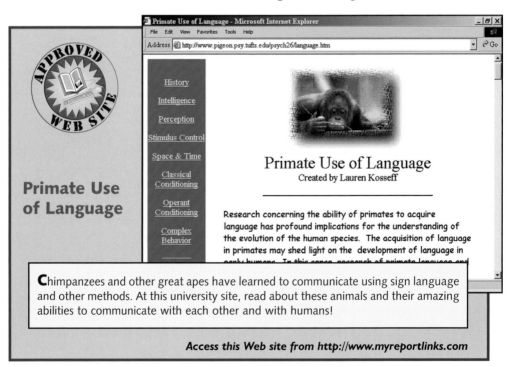

Primate Use of Language

Primate Use of Language - Microsoft Internet Explorer

File   Edit   View   Favorites   Tools   Help

Address http://www.pigeon.psy.tufts.edu/psych26/language.htm

History
Intelligence
Perception
Stimulus Control
Space & Time
Classical Conditioning
Operant Conditioning
Complex Behavior

Primate Use of Language
Created by Lauren Kosseff

Research concerning the ability of primates to acquire language has profound implications for the understanding of the evolution of the human species. The acquisition of language in primates may shed light on the development of language in early humans. In this sense, research of primate language and

Chimpanzees and other great apes have learned to communicate using sign language and other methods. At this university site, read about these animals and their amazing abilities to communicate with each other and with humans!

Access this Web site from http://www.myreportlinks.com

believed that the silence of chimpanzees could be overcome through sign language. He wrote, "I am inclined to conclude . . . that the great apes have plenty to talk about, but no gift for the use of sounds to represent individual . . . feelings or ideas. Perhaps they can be taught to use their fingers. . . ."[1]

Indeed, chimpanzees cannot use sounds as we can. They are unable to speak. We now know that there are differences in the vocal tracts of chimpanzees and humans. The vocal tract consists of cavities and structures in the vocal cords of animals and humans that can shape and change the flow of air and vibrations of sound. A chimpanzee cannot use its tongue to change the shape of the vocal tract as a human being can. The chimp cannot produce many of the same sounds that humans can. Nevertheless, some researchers were so impressed with the early work of Köhler and Yerkes testing chimpanzee intelligence that they were determined to find out whether chimps could speak.

Raising Chimpanzees in the Home

In 1931, a chimpanzee from Yerkes' laboratory was raised by psychologist Winthrop Kellogg in his home. The chimp, Gua, lived with Kellogg, his wife, Luella, and their young son, Donald. Both chimp and child, each the same age, were tested daily. The Kelloggs ended their experiment when they noticed that Donald was learning more chimpanzee sounds than Gua was learning human sounds. According to rumor, Donald was also making food grunts at the dinner table.

In 1947, psychologist Keith Hayes and his wife, Cathy, adopted a month-old chimpanzee named Viki. They brought Viki up in their own home, as if she were their own daughter. Viki was given several years of intensive language training. She was constantly encouraged to pick up words and imitate sounds. Viki was very intelligent and did well in intelligence tests. Apparently, Viki was able to communicate by using photos. She understood on some level that photos are pictures of real things. For example, when Viki wanted to go for a car ride, she would tear a photo of a car out of a magazine and hand it to Hayes. But by the time of her death, at just age six, Viki could only "speak" four words: *mama, papa, up,* and *cup.* Actually, Viki breathed rather than spoke the words. This failure prompted other researchers to try different approaches.

▷ Teaching Chimpanzees to Communicate Using ASL

In 1966, a psychologist-ethologist husband-wife team, Allen and Beatrice Gardner, acquired a one-year-old female chimpanzee named Washoe. The Gardners planned to follow Robert Yerkes' suggestion. They would attempt to teach Washoe to communicate by using her fingers. And it seemed that the most useful method would be to teach Washoe sign language.

The Gardners raised Washoe at their home in Reno, Nevada. But Washoe lived in a trailer in the backyard rather than in the Gardner's house. Apparently, the Gardners were good teachers, and Washoe proved to be a quick learner. Not only did she learn signs easily, but she also began to string them together in meaningful ways. The Gardners

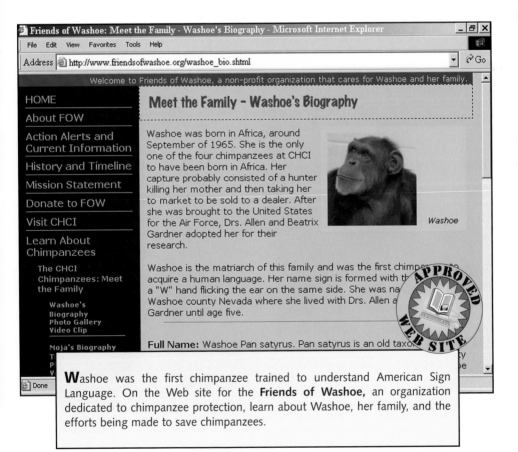

Washoe was the first chimpanzee trained to understand American Sign Language. On the Web site for the **Friends of Washoe,** an organization dedicated to chimpanzee protection, learn about Washoe, her family, and the efforts being made to save chimpanzees.

treated their chimpanzee like a human child, giving her a lot of affection, but they tested Washoe regularly in a strict, scientific manner. It became clear to them that each sign evoked in Washoe's mind an image of the object it repre- sented. For example, Allen or Beatrice Gardner, using sign language, would ask Washoe to fetch an apple. Washoe would go and get one, even if it was out of sight in another room.

▲ Chimpanzees show a curiosity about their environment that is rare in the animal kingdom.

The Gardners' project was a great success. In 1970, Washoe was sent to work with Roger Fouts at the Institute for Primate Studies in Oklahoma. By that time, Washoe was using 132 signs and could understand hundreds of others. Fouts had first met Washoe at a children's play yard on the campus of the University of Nevada-Reno. Washoe greeted Fouts by leaping into his arms and giving him a big hug. Allen Gardner was very pleased and hired Fouts as his assistant. Fouts worked with Washoe during the next few years as he completed his graduate studies.

▷ Other Teaching Methods

During the early 1970s, other scientists began teaching ASL to chimpanzees and other primates. Penny Patterson taught a gorilla named Koko to use ASL. Lynn Miles taught an orangutan named Chantek to use ASL.

Some researchers working with chimps in the laboratory tried a completely different approach. David and Ann Premack created an artificial language to teach a female chimp named Sarah to communicate. The Premacks used plastic pieces with metal backs on a magnetized board. The plastic pieces were of different sizes, shapes, and colors. Each piece was a symbol representing a word. The Premacks used the plastic symbols to ask Sarah a question. Sarah answered by placing the correct pieces in the correct order.

At the Yerkes Regional Primate Research Center in Atlanta, Georgia, Duane Rumbaugh created a computerized language he called "Yerkish." He taught Yerkish to a chimpanzee named Lana. Lana communicated by punching Yerkish symbols on a keyboard. Sue Savage-Rumbaugh used Yerkish with two chimps named Sherman and Austin and a bonobo named Kanzi.

In 1973, Herbert Terrace acquired an infant chimpanzee, whom he named Nim Chimpsky. This name was a humorous reference to the famous linguistics scholar Noam Chomsky. Most linguists, including Chomsky, thought that the idea of a chimpanzee learning language was absurd. Nevertheless, Terrace began his Project

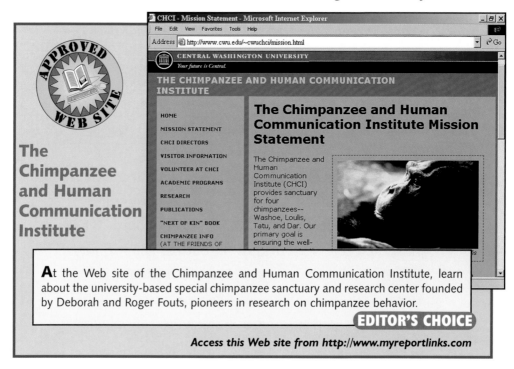

The Chimpanzee and Human Communication Institute

At the Web site of the Chimpanzee and Human Communication Institute, learn about the university-based special chimpanzee sanctuary and research center founded by Deborah and Roger Fouts, pioneers in research on chimpanzee behavior.

EDITOR'S CHOICE

Access this Web site from http://www.myreportlinks.com

Nim intending to teach the chimp ASL and prove that chimpanzees could create sentences. Terrace took a different approach from those of other ASL researchers. Instead of giving Nim love and affection, he provided none. Instead of surrounding Nim with things that might stimulate his curiosity, he kept him in a small, empty room during training. Terrace believed that Nim would concentrate better on language lessons if there were no distractions. Unfortunately, Project Nim was a failure, and Terrace concluded that chimpanzees could not create sentences.

Meaningful Signs

Meanwhile, back in Oklahoma, Roger Fouts continued working with Washoe. Washoe had often used signs in her own way, combining them in ways that were meaningful to her. For example, she had been taught POTTY CHAIR for "toilet," and COLD BOX for "refrigerator." But Washoe came up with DIRTY GOOD for "toilet," and OPEN FOOD DRINK for "refrigerator."

Washoe's sign combinations were never nonsensical. She only used signs that were relevant to the situation. For example, Washoe was given a test in which she needed help. Each time, Susan, a graduate student, would "accidentally" step on Washoe's doll. These were Washoe's reactions: UP SUSAN, SUSAN UP, MINE PLEASE UP, GIMME

BABY, PLEASE SHOE, MORE MINE, UP PLEASE, PLEASE UP, MORE UP, BABY DOWN, SHOE UP, BABY UP, PLEASE MORE UP, and YOU UP.[2]

A Family Expands

In 1979, Roger Fouts and his wife, Deborah, acquired a one-year-old male chimpanzee named Loulis from the Yerkes Regional Primate Research Center. Washoe adopted the infant as soon as she met him. Fouts and his wife purposely did not teach Loulis any signs. However, after eighteen months with Washoe, Loulis was using two dozen signs.

On many occasions, Fouts observed Washoe tutoring Loulis. One day, Washoe placed a chair in front of Loulis. She then showed him the CHAIR SIT sign five times. As Fouts recalled, "Another time, with Loulis watching, Washoe signed FOOD over and over when one of the volunteers brought her a bowl of oatmeal. Then Washoe molded Loulis's hand into the sign for FOOD and touched it to his mouth several times just as parents of deaf children often do."[3] Loulis became the first chimpanzee to learn ASL from another chimpanzee, the first nonhuman to learn a human language from another nonhuman.

Several other families in Norman, Oklahoma, were raising young chimpanzees in their homes. Fouts made regular visits to them, teaching the chimps ASL. One of the chimps, named Lucy,

▲ *A chimpanzee perches on a branch to eat. The first sign that Washoe taught Loulis was the sign for food. Loulis thus became the first chimpanzee to learn American Sign Language from another chimpanzee.*

belonged to Jane and Maury Temerlin. Lucy learned ASL and attempted to teach it to her pet cat. Maury Temerlin wrote about his chimpanzee "daughter" in his book *Lucy: Growing Up Human.*

Fouts now works with a community of chimpanzees, Washoe's family, at the Chimpanzee and Human Communication Institute at Central Washington University. The chimps communicate with their human caregivers and also with each other by using ASL. Adult chimpanzees in the group have passed the language on to their children.

CURRENT EFFORTS TO PROTECT THE CHIMPANZEE

Despite all these efforts to study chimps and even to teach them language, the chimpanzee as a species is in serious trouble. There are fewer than two hundred thousand chimpanzees left in their native African habitat. About two thousand chimpanzees live in captivity in biomedical facilities or zoos. If present trends continue, chimpanzees may become extinct.

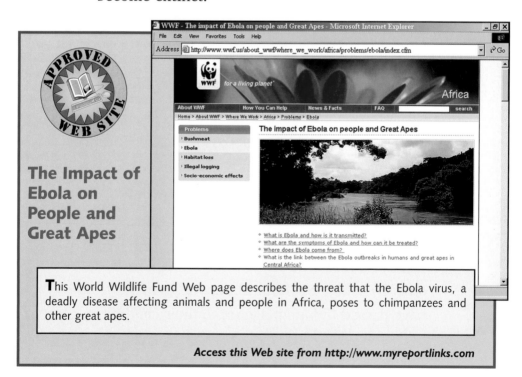

The Impact of Ebola on People and Great Apes

This World Wildlife Fund Web page describes the threat that the Ebola virus, a deadly disease affecting animals and people in Africa, poses to chimpanzees and other great apes.

Access this Web site from http://www.myreportlinks.com

▶ Threats Remain

Humans pose the greatest threat to chimpanzees. The forests of central Africa, where the chimps make their home, have been opened up by timber companies, who build logging roads. Those roads provide access for organized groups of hunters, who capture chimpanzee infants to sell as exotic pets or for entertainment uses. The roads also make it easier for poachers to hunt chimps and sell their meat in the illegal bush-meat trade.

Even the chimpanzees in the protected area of Gombe in Tanzania are threatened by the expansion of human activities and settlement. The chimps still roam free within the park, but their refuge is bordered by villages and cultivated land on three sides.

Disease is also a major threat facing the chimpanzees and other great apes in Africa. The deadly Ebola virus is spreading in central and western Africa. Like humans, chimpanzees suffer terribly from this disease, which is often fatal. In April 2005, conservationists and primatologists met in Washington, D.C., to discuss the crisis. They proposed vaccinating the great ape populations, but first, resources would need to be made available to develop an effective vaccine. Some promising work has already been done in laboratories. But it could take up to five years until vaccinations could begin. Another suggestion was to clear small rivers of overhanging trees. Chimps and other apes are reluctant to cross open water. Getting rid of tree branches will keep infected chimpanzees from crossing rivers, which may help keep the virus from spreading.

Chimpanzees, so like humans in their biology, can easily catch human diseases. But because chimps have not built up the same resistance, human diseases are far more deadly to chimps. How can chimpanzees catch such diseases? For one, the careless disposal of human waste in chimpanzee habitat has led to epidemics of tuberculosis, influenza, polio, and scabies in chimpanzees. Human disease can also be transmitted by people visiting chimpanzee sanctuaries. Visitors need to take precautions not to spread infection to the animals. They should not visit the sanctuaries if they are sick and should keep a distance from the chimps even if they are well.

▶ Great Apes on the Brink

Wildlife experts are concerned with how quickly chimpanzees and other great apes are declining in number. In 1998, Dr. Peter Walsh, a Princeton University scientist, led an international group of researchers to West Africa to survey great-ape populations. By 2002, they found that the population decline of these animals had increased dramatically. They predicted that if the current trend continues, the population will decline by

The **Wildlife Conservation Society** uses various methods, such as educational initiatives and scientific research, to protect the world's endangered species and habitats. Learn more about this organization and the work it is doing in Africa on its Web site.

another 80 percent within thirty years or even less time. Walsh's group wants gorillas and chimpanzees, currently listed as "endangered," to be listed as "critically endangered." According to Walsh, "The species that are most similar to humans are just disappearing before our eyes."[1]

▶ The Great Ape Project

The best hope for saving chimpanzees and other great apes may come from the courtroom. Roger and

Deborah Fouts serve on the board of the Great Ape Project (GAP). Its goal is to win legal rights for all nonhuman great apes. (By now, many scientists accept classifying humans as a particular kind of great ape.) To accomplish this goal, GAP has joined forces with the Animal Legal Defense Fund to create the Great Ape Legal Project. The project's strategy is to bring cases to court to get the judicial system to recognize that our closest relatives are "beings" that deserve legal protection.

The Great Ape Project has produced a Declaration on Great Apes. The declaration describes a community of equals that includes all the great apes, including human beings. The

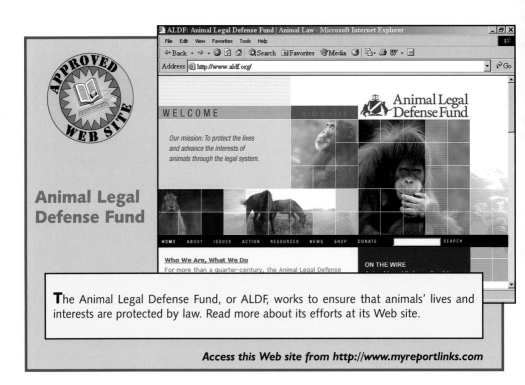

Animal Legal Defense Fund

The Animal Legal Defense Fund, or ALDF, works to ensure that animals' lives and interests are protected by law. Read more about its efforts at its Web site.

Access this Web site from http://www.myreportlinks.com

▲ *It is up to us, all of us, to ensure that chimpanzee mothers and babies survive for many years to come.*

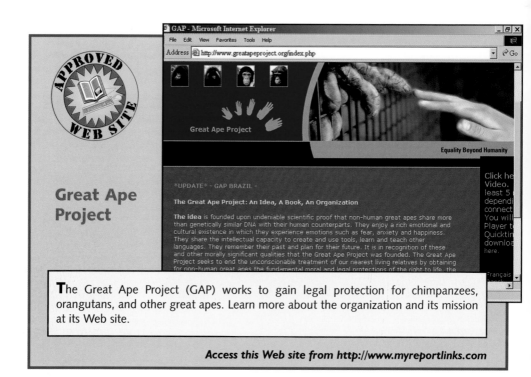

Great Ape Project

The Great Ape Project (GAP) works to gain legal protection for chimpanzees, orangutans, and other great apes. Learn more about the organization and its mission at its Web site.

Access this Web site from http://www.myreportlinks.com

declaration demands the following rights for all great apes: the right to life, the protection of individual liberty, and the prohibition of torture. The Great Ape Project's long-term goal is a United Nations Declaration of the Rights of Great Apes. Then GAP will push for the establishment of safe, guarded territories where the various nonhuman great apes can live and flourish. Humans have placed chimpanzees and other great apes on the brink of extinction. It is up to us, therefore, to make sure these incredible creatures, so like us and yet so different, do not disappear from our planet forever.

In 1973, Congress took the farsighted step of creating the Endangered Species Act, widely regarded as the world's strongest and most effective wildlife conservation law. It set an ambitious goal: to reverse the alarming trend of human-caused extinction that threatened the ecosystems we all share.

Each book in this series explores the life of an endangered animal. The books tell how and why the animals have become endangered and explain the efforts being made to restore their populations.

The United States Fish and Wildlife Service and the National Marine Fisheries Service share responsibility for administration of the Endangered Species Act. Over time, animals are added to, reclassified in, or removed from the federal list of Endangered and Threatened Wildlife and Plants. At the time of publication, all the animals in this series were listed as endangered species. The most up-to-date list can be found at **http://www.fws.gov/ endangered/wildlife.html**.

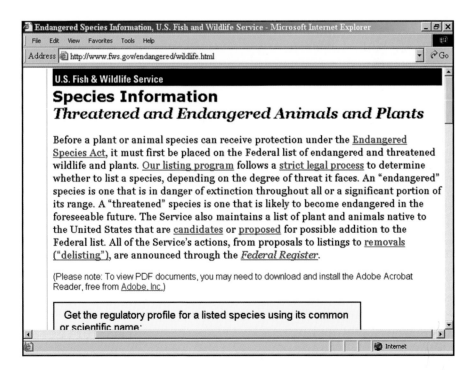

The Internet sites described below can be accessed at http://www.myreportlinks.com

▶**The Jane Goodall Institute for Wildlife Research, Education and Conservation**
Editor's Choice Find out about chimpanzee conservation from the Web site of the Jane Goodall Institu◄

▶**Save the Chimps**
Editor's Choice Learn about the efforts of this organization to rescue chimps.

▶**Wolfgang Köhler Primate Research Center**
Editor's Choice Learn about the conservation efforts of the Wolfgang Köhler Primate Research Cent◄

▶**Roots & Shoots**
Editor's Choice You can become involved in saving the world and its species through Roots & Shoots.

▶**Lessons for Hope**
Editor's Choice A program of the Jane Goodall Institute offers hope for the world and all its species◄

▶**The Chimpanzee and Human Communication Institute**
Editor's Choice This institute protects chimps and fosters "responsible stewardship of the Earth."

▶**Animal Diversity Web: *Pan troglodytes* (chimpanzee)**
Browse through this comprehensive fact sheet about chimpanzees.

▶**Animal Legal Defense Fund**
Read about a group whose mission is to protect the lives and interests of animals through the legal syst◄

▶**Animal Planet: Jane Goodall**
Explore this Web site devoted to Jane Goodall and the chimpanzees of Gombe.

▶**Caring for Chimpanzees: The Chimpanzee Species Survival Plan**
Information about the chimpanzee species survival plan can be found on this zoo site.

▶**ChimpanZoo: Grooming**
Learn the facts about the grooming behavior of chimpanzees.

▶**Chimp Haven: Facts About Chimpanzees**
Find brief facts about chimpanzees on this rescue organization's Web site.

▶**Columbus Zoo and Aquarium: Bonobo**
Get information on the chimpanzee's cousin, the bonobo, on the Columbus Zoo and Aquarium Web site.

▶***Creature Feature: Chimpanzees***
An interactive feature about chimpanzees is offered on this *National Geographic Kids* Web site.

▶**ESPECIES Fact Sheets**
This Defenders of Wildlife site provides facts about chimpanzees.

Report Links

The Internet sites described below can be accessed at
http://www.myreportlinks.com

▶**The Fauna Foundation**
A sanctuary in Quebec, Canada, provides a dignified retirement for former lab chimps.

▶**Friends of Washoe**
Read about the Friends of Washoe and their chimpanzee conservation efforts.

▶**Great Ape Project**
Visit the Web site of the Great Ape Project, an organization dedicated to protecting the rights of apes.

▶**The Impact of Ebola on People and Great Apes**
Learn about the deadly Ebola virus and its effects on apes and humans.

▶**International Primate Protection League**
Find out about the International Primate Protection League's efforts to safeguard primates.

▶**Introduction to Human Evolution**
Information about the history of human evolution can be found on this site.

▶**JGI Center for Primate Studies**
Take a tour of Gombe, the Tanzanian national park made famous by Jane Goodall's work with

▶**The Leakey Foundation**
The Leakey Foundation, named for the renowned anthropologist, continues his work.

▶*Nature: Chimpanzees: An Unnatural History*
A PBS series profiles some unsung heroes who provide sanctuary for chimps.

▶**The Primates: Apes**
Visit this Web site for facts about chimpanzees and other great apes.

▶**Primate Use of Language**
This site discusses the abilities of primates to communicate with language.

▶**Project Primate, Inc.**
Explore the Web site of an organization dedicated to saving orphaned chimps in West Africa.

▶**USFWS Endangered Species Program Kid's Corner**
This USFWS Web site offers ways you can help save endangered species.

▶**Wildlife Conservation Society**
The Wildlife Conservation Society Web site offers information on endangered species.

▶**Write Your Representative**
Find links to your congressional representatives on this government site.

alpha male—The dominant male of a chimpanzee community.

altruism—Behavior that shows concern for others or benefits others.

anthropologist—A scientist who studies the origin and evolution of human beings.

biomedical—Relating to biological, medical, and physical science.

bonobo—A separate species of chimpanzee, sometimes called the pygmy chimpanzee.

brachiating—Traveling through the trees, swinging from branch to branch.

bush meat—The meat of wild animals that is sold illegally.

charging display—A threatening action by a male chimpanzee.

consortship—An exclusive short-term relationship between a male chimpanzee and a female chimpanzee.

deforestation—The process of clearing forests of trees for timber, development, to build roads, and so on.

dominance—In the animal world, an individual or group with power over another.

encroach—To advance into an area belonging to another.

ethology—The scientific study of animal behavior.

evolution—In biology, the process of change by which new species form from existing species over time. This change comes through natural selection, in which the organisms best adapted to their environment survive over generations while those less well adapted do not.

fossil fuels—Fuels such as oil, natural gas, and coal that form in the ground from the remains of dead animals and plants.

genus—A group of closely related species.

habitat—The place where an animal or a plant normally lives.

home range—The area in which an animal eats, sleeps, and performs other daily activities.

indigenous—Native to an area, such as plants.

omnivore—An animal that eats plants and meat.

opposable—Referring to a thumb or toe, one that is capable of being placed against one or more other digits of a hand or foot.

presenting—A crouching posture taken by a low-ranking chimpanzee when greeting a higher-up.

primates—A group of mammals that includes humans, greater apes (chimpanzees, bonobos, gorillas, and orangutans), lesser apes (gibbons and siamangs), baboons, monkeys, and animals such as lemurs and marmosets.

savannas—Large areas of grassy African plains.

species—A group of organisms so similar to one another that they can interbreed.

subordinate—Belonging to a lower class or rank; a lower member in a social hierarchy.

Chapter 1. Our Closest Relative

1. Jane Goodall, *Through a Window—My Thirty Years with the Chimpanzees of Gombe* (Boston: Houghton-Mifflin, 1990), p. 19; quoted in *Rattling the Cage: Towards Legal Rights for Animals* by Steven M. Wise (Cambridge, Mass.: Perseus Publishing, 2000), p. 191.

2. Roger Fouts, *Next of Kin* (New York: William Morrow and Company, Inc., 1997), p. 95.

3. *The Chimpanzee Collaboratory,* n.d., <http://www.chimpcollaboratory.org> (July 31, 2006).

Chapter 2. About Chimpanzees

1. Jane Goodall, *The Chimpanzees of Gombe: Patterns of Behavior* (Cambridge, Mass.: Harvard University Press, 1986), p. 6.

Chapter 3. Chimpanzee Behavior

1. Jane Goodall, *The Chimpanzees of Gombe: Patterns of Behavior* (Cambridge, Mass.: Harvard University Press, 1986), p. 255.

2. Ibid., p. 535.

3. *Save the Chimps,* n.d., <http://savethechimps.org> (July 31, 2006).

4. Goodall, p. 127.

Chapter 4. Early Research

1. Roger Fouts, *Next of Kin* (New York: William Morrow and Company, Inc., 1997), p. 50.

2. Ibid., p. 48.

3. Edward Tyson, *The Anatomy of a Pygmie* (London, 1699); quoted in *The Chimpanzees of Gombe: Patterns of Behavior* by Jane Goodall (Cambridge, Mass.: Harvard University Press, 1986), p. 6.

4. C.E. Hoppius, *Anthropomorpha. Amoenitates*

academicae (Linne), erlangae, 1789; quoted in *The Chimpanzees of Gombe: Patterns of Behavior* by Jane Goodall (Cambridge, Mass.: Harvard University Press, 1986), p. 5.

5. Jennifer Lindsey, *The Great Apes* (New York: Friedman/Fairfax Publishers, 1999), p. 13.

6. Wolfgang Köhler, *The Mentality of Apes* (New York: Harcourt, Brace & Company, Inc., 1925), p. 1, as quoted on the Web site of the Wolfgang Köhler Primate Research Center, *Memoir,* n.d., <http://wkprc.eva.mpg.de/english/files/wolfgang_koehler.htm> (July 31, 2006).

7. Frans B.M. de Waal, "The Evolution of Empathy," p. 7, *Greater Good,* a publication of the Center for the Development of Peace and Well-Being, the University of California, Berkeley, Fall/Winter 2005/6, <http://peacecenter.berkeley.edu/greatergood/archive/2005fallwinter/FallWinter0506_deWaal.pdf> (October 10, 2006).

8. Ibid.

Chapter 5. Jane Goodall and the Chimpanzees of Gombe

1. Mary G. Smith, *The Great Apes: Between Two Worlds* (Washington, D.C.: National Geographic Society, 1993), p. 30.

2. Wolfgang Köhler, *The Mentality of Apes* (New York: Harcourt, Brace & Company, Inc., 1925), p. 255; as quoted in *The Chimpanzees of Gombe: Patterns of Behavior* by Jane Goodall, (Cambridge, Mass.: Harvard University Press, 1986), p. 374.

Chapter 6. Chimpanzee-Human Communication

1. Mary G. Smith, *The Great Apes: Between Two Worlds* (Washington, D.C.: National Geographic Society, 1993), p. 39.

2. Roger Fouts, *Next of Kin* (New York: William Morrow and Company, Inc., 1997), p. 102.

3. Ibid., p. 244.

Chapter 7. Current Efforts to Protect the Chimpanzee

1. Peter Walsh, as quoted in Steven Schultz, "Wild Ape Population Undergoing 'Catastrophic' Decline," *Princeton Weekly Bulletin,* April 14, 2003, vol. 92, no. 23.

Bow, Patricia. *Chimpanzee Rescue: Changing the Future for Endangered Wildlife.* Buffalo: Firefly Books, 2004.

De Waal, Frans B.M. *The Ape and the Sushi Master: Cultural Reflections by a Primatologist.* New York: Basic Books, 2001.

Gilders, Michelle A. *The Nature of Great Apes: Our Next of Kin.* New York: Greystone Books, 2000.

Goodall, Jane. *The Chimpanzees I Love: Saving Their World and Ours.* New York: Scholastic Press, 2001.

————. *Through a Window: My Thirty Years with the Chimpanzees of Gombe.* Boston: Houghton Mifflin Company, 1990.

Greenberg, Daniel. *Chimpanzees.* New York: Marshall Cavendish, 2001.

Haugen, Brenda. *Jane Goodall: Legendary Zoologist.* Minneapolis: Compass Point Books, 2006.

Siddle, Sheila, with Doug Cress. *In My Family Tree: A Life With Chimpanzees.* New York: Grove Press, 2002.

Sloan, Christopher. *The Human Story: Our Evolution From Prehistoric Ancestors to Today.* Washington, D.C.: National Geographic, 2004.

Stefoff, Rebecca. *The Primate Order.* New York: Marshall Cavendish Benchmark, 2005.

A

adopt-a-chimp programs
  The Fauna Foundation, 20–22
  Save the Chimps, 23
aggression, 89–93
alpha males, 7, 54, 89, 90, 93
altruistic behaviors, 93–99
American Sign Language (ASL),
    7, 12, 100, 102–109
anatomy of chimpanzees,
    70–72, *96*
ants as diet, 45–46

B

baby chimps, 66–67. *See also*
    child raising.
behaviors
  aggression, 89–93
  altruism, 93–99
  differences among chimp
      species, 30–31
  emotions, 77, 79
  overview, 11–12, 52
  patterns of, 52–54
  research on, 75–80
  territoriality, 90
Boesch, Christoph, 46
bonobos, 13, 30
bush meat, 15

C

calls. *See* communication.
cannibalism, 92
caring for the sick, 99
child raising, *47, 64–65,* 66–67
Chimpanzee and Human
    Communication Institute, 12
Chimpanzee Collaboratory, 24
Chimpanzee Conservation
    Center, 22
chimpanzees
  described, 6, 28–30, 33–37
  as pets, 20–21, 33–34
  viewpoints on, 68–72
Chimp Guardian, 18
CITES, 14

communication
  ASL (*See* American Sign
      Language (ASL))
  and dominance, 54
  overview, 7, 35, 53, 100–101
  research on, 102–109
  verbal, 100–102
  via body language, 56–57
  via symbols, 105–106
  vocal, 57–63
community organization
  alpha males, 7, 54, 89, 90, 93
  dominance in, 54
  family units, 49, 52
  home range of, 48
  overview, 6–7, 46–47
  parties, 48–49
  relationships within, 52, 54
  wars and, 90–93
conflict resolution, 57
conservation, 110
  The Fauna Foundation, 19–22
  Great Ape Project, 113–116
  The Jane Goodall Institute for
      Wildlife Research,
      Education and
      Conservation, 16–18,
      21–22
  Save the Chimps, 22–23
  Wildlife Conservation
      Society, 113
consortships, 49, 66
Coulston Foundation, 22

D

Darwin, Charles, 72–75
development, 14–15
diet
  ants in, 45–46
  cannibalism, 92
  described, 6, 30–31, 38
  fruit in, 46
  research on, 88
  termites, fishing for, 38–45

E

Ebola virus, 111–112

education
    by citizens, 26–27
    by organizations, 16–27
emotional behaviors, 77–80. *See also* aggression; play.
Endangered Species Act of 1973
    endangered defined, 14
    supporting, 26–27
    threatened species defined, 14
entertainment industry, 16, 24, 69
evolution, 13–14, 71–75
exotic pet trade, 15

F
family units, 49, 52, *64–65*
The Fauna Foundation, 19–22
feeding habits, 48, 49, 60, 97–99
Fouts, Roger
    on chimp evolution, 13–14
    on chimp mental behaviors, 12
    communication research by, 102–109
    Great Ape Project, 113–116

G
Gardner, Allen and Beatrice, 102–105
gestation period, 7, 63, 66
global warming, 26
Gombe Stream National Park, 11, 18, 33, 45, 87. *See also* Goodall, Jane.
Goodall, Jane
    breakthrough by, 88–89
    on *chimpanzee* as taxonomic name, 28–29
    on chimp tool use, 40–41
    first contact with chimpanzees, 86–88
    Gombe, establishment of, 33
    history of, 84–86
    organizations started by, 16–19
    overview, 9, 11–12, 81–84

photograph of, *83*
    on vocal communication, 57
gracile chimpanzees, 13, 30
Great Ape Project, 113–116
grooming, 45, 54, 56, 63

H
habitat, 6, 31–32
habitat loss, 14–15, 26
hands described, *96*
Hoppius, C. E., 71–72
how to help this species survive. *See also* threats to survival.
    adopt-a-chimp programs (*See adopt-a-chimp programs*)
    education, providing, 24–25
    letter-writing campaigns, 26–27
    organizations, supporting, 16 (*See also specific organizations*)
hunting, 15–16
Huxley, Thomas, 72

I
inbreeding, 15
Itani, Junichiro, 82

J
Jane Goodall Institute for Wildlife Research, Education and Conservation, 16–18, 21–22

K
Köhler, Wolfgang, *74,* 75–77, 97, 99
Kohts, Nadia, 77, 79
Kortlandt, Adriaan, 81–82

L
Leakey, Louis, 11, 82, 84–85
life span, 6, 34–35
locomotion, 7, 35, *50–51, 60*

M
mating behaviors, 48–49, 58, 59, *62,* 63
medical experiments, 19–20, 22
memory in chimps, 57, 76
Meunier, Victor, 74–75
mixed parties, 49

N
Nissen, Henry, 80
nursery units, 49, 52

P
pant-grunt call, 58, 59
pant-hoot call, 58, 61
play
    laughing in, 37, 59
    as learning tool, 52
    by males, 45
    toy donations for, 23
    types of, 59
population decline, 112–113
population growth (human), 14–15
population statistics, 6, 25
presenting posture, 56
problem-solving skills
    research on, 75–77, 79
    tool use (*See* tool use)
Project Nim, 106–107
Project Primate, Inc., 21, 22
pygmy chimpanzee, 25

R
range, *5,* 6, *29*
reproduction, 7, 63, 66. *See also* gestation period; mating behaviors.
research
    altruistic behaviors, 93–99
    behaviors, 75–77
    Charles Darwin, 72–75
    on communication, 102–109
    on diet, 88
    emotional behaviors, 77–80
    history of, 68–72, 81–82

by Jane Goodall (*See* Goodall, Jane)
risk taking, 93–97
robust chimpanzees, 13, 30
Roots & Shoots, 18–19

S
Save the Chimps, 22–23
screams, 58, 59, 61, 63
sensory systems, 7, 35
size statistics, 6

T
taxonomy, 6, 29–30
termites, fishing for, 38–45
Terrace, Herbert, 106–107
threats to survival. *See also* how to help this species survive.
    development, 14–15
    disease, 111–112
    global warming, 26
    habitat loss, 14–15, 26
    human activities, 111
    hunting, 15–16
    inbreeding, 15
    overview, 7, 14–16
    population decline, 112–113
    population growth (human), 14–15
tool use
    overview, 7, 38–46
    research on, 11, 76, 88
Tyson, Edward, 70–71

W
war among chimps, 89–93
Washoe, 102–108
whimpers, 58, 59, 63
Wildlife Conservation Society, 113
Wolfgang Köhler Primate Research Center, 74

Y
Yerkes, Robert, 79–80, 100–101
Yerkish, 106